IMAGES
of America

SUGAR CREEK

Four members of the Cairns Busters girls' softball team must have been happy with the outcome of their game when this photograph was taken in 1939 or 1940. The young women in front of the team bus are, from left to right, (front) Lorene Allen; (standing) Frances Diesko, Annie Pallo, and Katie Zorich. The team bus, owned by team sponsor Ellis Cairns, was also used to transport Sugar Creek School students to and from school. Lorene Allen, known today as Lorene Lass, became the dominant organizer, collector, and conserver of all things Sugar Creek and the major influence for the creation of the Friends of Sugar Creek and the Sugar Creek Historical Center.

On the Cover: Street superintendent Edwin C. "Pete" Saxton (left) and Mayor Rudy J. Roper (right) discuss the progress being made on the construction of Sugar Creek's new community meeting and banquet center with head bricklayer Jim Callahan in this photograph taken in 1968 or 1969. The building would be named in honor of Mike D. Onka, the town's marshal who was killed in the line of duty in 1968. The dog sitting on the stone tree ring is Brownie, a neighbor's pet who had adopted Saxton and seldom left his side.

IMAGES
of America

SUGAR CREEK

Richard N. Piland for the
Sugar Creek Historical Center

ARCADIA
PUBLISHING

Published by Arcadia Publishing
Charleston, South Carolina

Library of Congress Control Number: 2009943881

For all general information, please contact Arcadia Publishing:
Telephone 843-853-2070
Fax 843-853-0044
E-mail sales@arcadiapublishing.com
For customer service and orders:
Toll-Free 1-888-313-2665

Visit us on the Internet at www.arcadiapublishing.com

This book is dedicated to the Creekers who attended Van Horn High School with me during the late 1950s and early 1960s. It was a distinct pleasure to have known the young men and women who would later become Sugar Creek's aldermen, city officials, business leaders, and community assets. I am proud to call them my friends.

CONTENTS

Acknowledgments   6

Introduction   7

1.   Early Days   9

2.   Serving the Community   27

3.   Business and Industry   43

4.   Building Sound Minds   63

5.   Tending Souls   77

6.   Standard Oil   89

7.   Community Life   109

ACKNOWLEDGMENTS

This book was made possible by the work, commitment, and devotion of Lorene Lass in saving the history of Sugar Creek. Without her effort, there would be no photographic collection or archival resources at the Sugar Creek Historical Center for me to use to develop this record. In fact, without her tireless effort there would not even be a historical center. She has put in immeasurable time, work, and personal funds to gather, organize, store, and preserve all of the contributions to the center to produce a wonderful gift to the community.

I would also like to thank the board of directors of the Friends of Sugar Creek for giving me unlimited access to the historical center's photograph collection and archives. The support for the project given by Charley Dumsky, Joy Eaton, Roger Hooper, Lorene Lass, Jody Thomas, and Steve Topi is greatly appreciated. I want to also give a very special thank-you to Joy Eaton, Charley Dumsky, Steve Topi, and Marge Rucker for their help and patience when I scanned the photographs at the historical center.

Most of the photographs included in this book are found in the collection at the Sugar Creek Historical Center at 606 North Sterling Avenue, Sugar Creek, Missouri, 64054. Where that is not the case, the contributor of the image is noted. I would like to thank the following for the photographs they donated: Laurel Ann Bonine, Al Carlisle, Joy Eaton, Leigh Ann Little, Matt Mallinson, Doris Snyder, Jim Steele, Steve Topi, and Phyllis White. I regret that I was unable to use all the images I was offered.

Several people helped me with background information about Sugar Creek and its history. I am grateful to Cliff Braden; Earle Conner; Charley Dumsky; Jane, John, and Matt Mallinson; Ron Martinovich; Donna Newton; Herb Soule; and Steve Topi for their help in sorting out historical events and putting names with faces. I am especially indebted to two publications for providing invaluable background information: the *Golden Memories of the City of Sugar Creek*, a 28-page booklet edited by Bill Allison and prepared for the town's 50th anniversary in 1970, and *The Illustrated History of Fairmount Park* by John M. Olinskey, Debra Topi, and Leigh Ann Little, an online book viewable at www.oldfairmountpark.com. I also wish to thank Anna Wilson and John Pearson at Arcadia Publishing for their support, commitment, and efforts in finding ways to solve the problems I presented them.

Finally, I want to acknowledge the support and understanding of my wife, Marcy. She has always been a source of constant love and encouragement for me as we travel life together.

INTRODUCTION

The first settlement in what is now Sugar Creek was at the steamboat port on the Missouri River first known as Upper Independence Landing, where supplies and passengers arrived during the 1840s and 1850s for the overland trip west from nearby Independence on the Santa Fe, California, and Oregon Trails. The port was renamed Wayne City Landing after Lt. Anthony Wayne, who had camped on the bluffs overlooking the river in 1825 while keeping the Kaw Indians confined to their land in Kansas.

The first railroad west of the Mississippi River was built in 1850 to join the river port and the Independence town square. It operated over 4 miles of wooden rails with flatcars drawn by mules that pulled supplies and pioneers from the landing through Sugar Creek to Independence before being abandoned in 1852 and replaced by a macadamized road by 1856. The entire Sugar Creek area remained heavily wooded with a few farms, pastures, and orchards. By 1877, all of the land surrounding the creek was dotted with a dozen farms ranging in size from 16 to 220 acres.

In 1891, Arthur E. Stillwell, a Kansas City railroad man, purchased 70 of the 160 acres of land owned by J. D. Cusenberry. Stillwell, who owned the Kansas City and Independence Air Line electric trolley, founded a first-class pleasure resort on the property in the southern part of Sugar Creek that would be popular until the 1930s. Fairmount Park's attractions included a spring-fed lake for boating and swimming, picnic grounds, a hotel, rental cabins, café, theater, Ferris wheel, merry-go-round, roller coaster, dancing pavilion, and a wide variety of other entertaining venues.

Standard Oil of Indiana purchased 70 acres of land at the north end of Sugar Creek in 1903 for a new refinery. The company had been formed in Whiting, Indiana, by industrialist John D. Rockefeller as part of the Standard Oil trust in 1889. Construction of the refinery began in March, and the promise of steady employment and a new community attracted rugged men to the area, many with Slovak or Croatian cultural backgrounds. The company brought a nucleus of operating and mechanical employees from its Whiting facility to staff the new refinery. By October 1904, the company had produced and shipped its first product—kerosene used to light lamps and heat cookstoves.

In March 1904, a group of 10 investors formed the Sugar Creek Townsite Company and raised $30,000 to purchase much of the land surrounding the Standard Oil property, mostly on the south side of the facility. The land was divided and sold for homesites, streets were planned, and residential construction began in earnest. Since there was no municipal government, town site residents relied on the refinery to provide firefighting services and water and sewage facilities. The earliest developments in the community included the start of three churches and building a four-room school. For many years, Sugar Creek's continued growth evolved around the refinery.

Shortly after World War I, businessmen and community leaders formed the Sugar Creek Improvement Association to hasten development by installing streetlights, paving streets, and improving the overall quality of life in the community. By 1920, the refinery had expanded, several new businesses had opened, many new homes had been built, and the population had grown to about 1,800. The improvement association petitioned the Jackson County Court for incorporation as a city, and on November 15, 1920, the court approved the request and appointed the town's first mayor and city government.

Community development and overall prosperity characterized the decade of the 1920s. City government focused on solving problems related to a public water supply, sanitation facilities, and sewers. The old school building was expanded, and an additional new building was added to the facility. A volunteer fire department was established, and the town's first two fire trucks were purchased. Streets were resurfaced, renamed, and given new lighting; and a new city hall was built.

For the next several decades, life in Sugar Creek would mirror that in most American small towns. Problems brought on by the Great Depression included liquidation of the town's only bank. Residents experienced a Spartan life during World War II, which claimed several of the town's bravest. Following the war, the town experienced a period of steady and substantial growth.

During the 1950s, the city built a large municipal swimming pool and a new elementary school and dedicated the William Henry Harrison Memorial Park. In 1958, the city grew for the first time with the annexation of about 285 acres to the south and east. The next decade saw the town build a new city hall, a police and fire building, a sewage treatment plant, and a community activities center. A 1964 annexation added about 2,300 acres to the town and brought the Missouri Portland Cement Company and Chevron Chemical Company into the city.

Over the years, much of the community's well-being depended upon the success of the Standard Oil refinery. The Amoco Oil Company (formerly Standard Oil of Indiana) stunned the community when it announced it would close down the plant by June 1982 due to declining demand for petroleum products in the United States. Almost amazingly, the town has survived the loss of the refinery that so dominated life in the community for nearly 80 years.

Readers are invited to take a pictorial journey through Sugar Creek's history to see who came here first, what they did, and how they worked to make the town a wonderful community for family, friends, and fun and a special place where life is a little sweeter.

One

EARLY DAYS

The Missouri General Assembly created Jackson County in 1826 and named Independence the county seat the following year. Much early growth in the county occurred around Independence, which became an agricultural center for the area and the starting point for the westward migration over the Santa Fe, Oregon, and California Trails. In 1850, a 4-mile railroad, the first built west of the Mississippi River, transported supplies and travelers from the landing at Wayne City through Sugar Creek to the Independence town square.

During the 1850s and over the next several decades, Sugar Creek was essentially a few farms, pastures, and orchards. An 1877 Jackson County atlas indicates the area had a dozen farms ranging in size from 16 to 220 acres. In 1891, J. D. Cusenberry, owner of 160 acres in the southern part of the area, sold part of his property to Arthur E. Stillwell, an enterprising Kansas City railroad man who had started the Kansas City and Independence Airline Railroad. Stillwell began to develop his land by building an earthen dam that created an 18-acre lake. He laid out picnic grounds, added a pavilion, bandstand, carousel, shooting gallery, and other attractions. In 1892, he opened Cusenberry Springs as a pleasure resort to provide Kansas City area residents with an escape and another reason to use his electric trolley. After the first year of operation, Stillwell renamed his resort Fairmount Park.

Over the next 40 years, Fairmount Park's attractions included the large lake for boating and swimming, picnic grounds, a hotel, rental cabins, café, outdoor theater, Ferris wheel, merry-go-round, roller coasters, zoo, dancing pavilion, and a wide variety of entertainment venues. Patrons saw some of the best vaudeville acts in the country, watched early films, and were entertained by all sorts of displays, exhibitions, and spectacles. The park would be a popular local destination until the 1930s.

In 1903, Standard Oil of Indiana purchased 70 acres of land at the north end of Sugar Creek for a new refinery. Construction of the refinery brought various rugged men to the area, many with Slovak or Croatian cultural backgrounds. By October 1904, the company had produced and shipped its first product—kerosene used to light lamps and heat cookstoves.

In March 1904, several investors formed the Sugar Creek Townsite Company and purchased much of the land surrounding the refinery. The land was divided into homesites, and residential construction began. Since there was no municipal government, residents relied upon the refinery to provide many of their needs. For many years, Sugar Creek's growth would revolve around the refinery.

The first settlement in what is now Sugar Creek was at Wayne City Landing, the Missouri River port where merchandise and supplies were received and then taken to Independence for outfitting overland journeys to the West. Wayne City was established in 1845 and platted in 1847. This engraving from an 1877 county atlas shows the farm and warehouse built on the original river landing site after it was acquired in 1866 by Robert and Maria Turner. The area was designated an historic site by Sugar Creek's board of aldermen in 1983. (Jackson County Historical Society.)

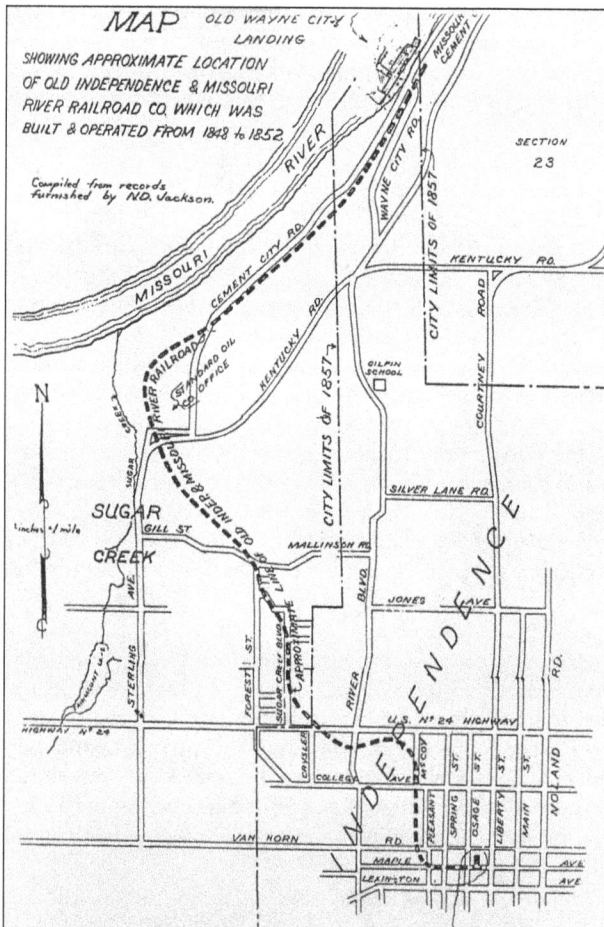

Construction of the Independence and Missouri River Railroad began in 1848. Between 1850 and 1852, the wooden rails of the mule-powered railroad moved people and freight for westward migration up from Wayne City Landing through Sugar Creek to Independence along the route indicated in this map. The railroad was abandoned in 1852 after a sandbar at the landing diverted boat traffic upriver to Kansas City.

Oliver James Dickey was one of the earliest settlers of the Sugar Creek area. He was a Civil War veteran who had fought with the 79th Pennsylvania Volunteers Regiment of the Army of the Cumberland during several battles, including Green River, Kentucky; Stones River near Murfreesboro, Tennessee; and Chattanooga, Tennessee, in 1861 through 1863. In 1880, Dickey built one of the first houses in Sugar Creek, the modest home seen in the photograph below. The house was located on what would be named Elizabeth Street. In 1889, Dickey built a larger residence for his family on the same street. Dickey died in 1905 and his wife, Caroline, died in 1936.

James Mallinson was among the earliest settlers of the Sugar Creek area when he moved to the county in 1859. Three generations of his family are seen on the steps leading up from the river at the old Wayne City Landing in this photograph taken around 1910. From left to right they are (first row) John William Mallinson and his father, Abraham Mallinson (James's eldest son); (second row) Caroline Hagen Mallinson (James's widow) and Effie Rockey Mallinson (Abraham's wife).

Fairmount Park was called Cusenberry Springs when it was founded by Arthur Stillwell and opened for business during the late spring 1892. Stillwell was a well-known Kansas City railroad man who also owned the Air Line electric trolley line that brought people to the park's entrance gate seen in this image. The park stretched northward from Independence Avenue, between Northern Boulevard and Sterling Avenue, all the way to Kentucky Avenue.

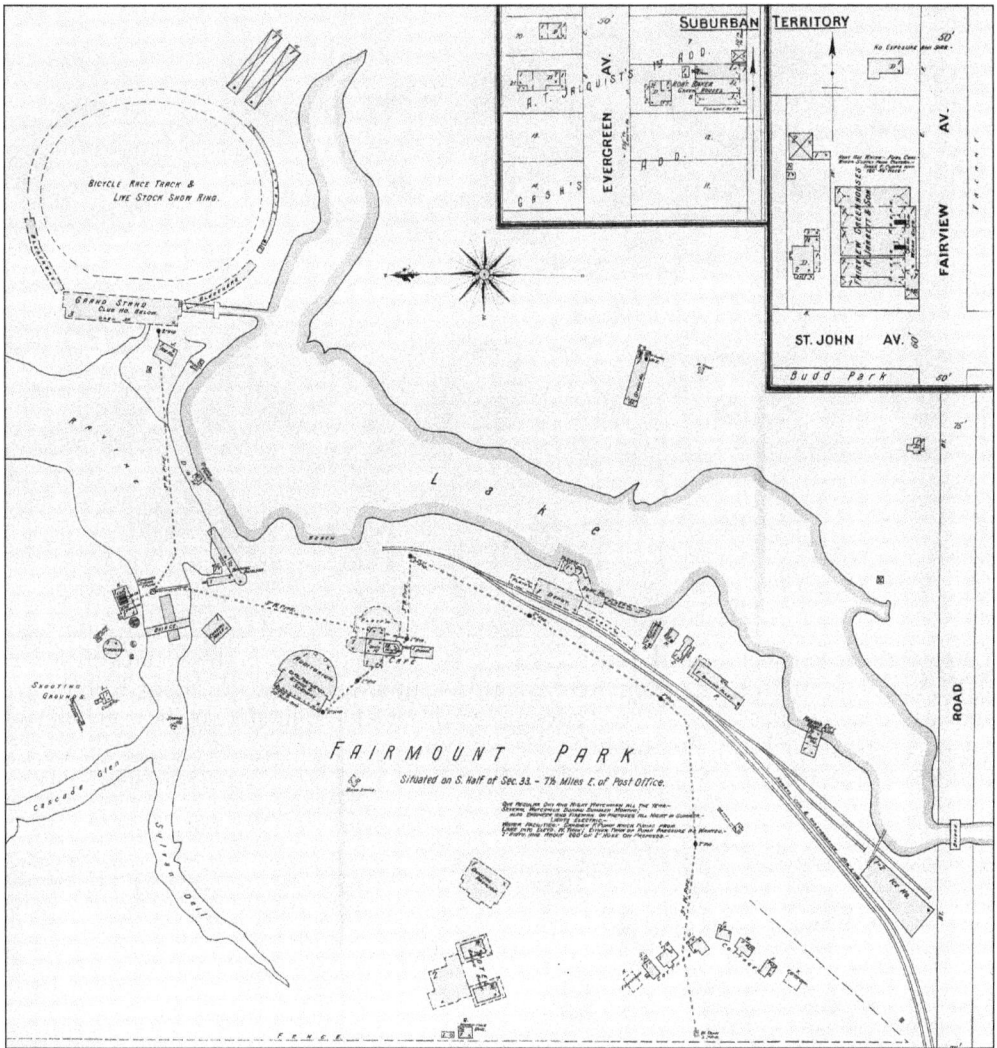

A Sanborn Fire Insurance map shows Fairmount Park in 1896. In the upper left is the northeast corner of the park with a bicycle racetrack and livestock show ring. In 1893, Arthur Stillwell started the Fairmount Cycling Club at the track; it evolved into the Kansas City Athletic Club. The oval was the site of several horse shows beginning in 1895, which became the American Royal by 1905. Attractions near the center include a 90-foot diving tower, bathing pavilion, beach, Crystal Maze hall of mirrors, café, dining room, and auditorium. On the opposite side of the bridge are a carousel, skeet shooting grounds, and Cascade Glen, a lovers' lane. On the lake side of the trolley tracks and depot are the rental boathouse, electric theater, shooting gallery, and bowling alley. Nearby is the boathouse for the Kansas City Boat Club. The lower portion shows a dancing pavilion, the Fairmount Hotel, and rental cabins under construction. To the far right is Independence Avenue. (University of Missouri Ellis Library Special Collections.)

This artist's rendering of the park's attractions and layout shows many of the features offered in 1897. Admission was free, but patrons were charged for entrance to most attractions, bathing suit and boat rentals, food, and most rides. Patrons also paid fares for Stillwell's electric trolley to and from the park. (Laurel Ann Bonine.)

By 1893, a new dock on the lake was finished. Charles Carlisle operated a boat rental business and was also responsible for managing the boathouse, beach, and fishing. Every year, boats were repaired, repainted, and upgraded or replaced as new equipment became available. Carlisle also restocked the lake with fish, rented out fishing poles and supplies, and maintained the sandy beach used by the public. Carlisle Avenue was named in his honor. (Al Carlisle.)

14

This photograph from 1924 shows several groups of people canoeing on the lake, a portion of the dock to the left, and the picnic grounds beyond the water's edge. The lake was also used for boat races, swimming, and as a landing area for parachutists who jumped from hot-air balloons high over the park. In the evenings, the lake hosted spectacular fireworks displays and elaborate reenactments of naval battles fought during the Civil War or Spanish-American War. (Al Carlisle.)

The high-dive platform, seen in this 1900 photograph, was located at the north end of the lake on top of the earthen dam. It rose 90 feet above the water. In 1893, Joseph Leuvenmark, a champion diver from Stockholm, Sweden, set the first of several world records he established with dives at the lake. Daily diving exhibitions were held during the park's early years but were discontinued sometime before 1909. (Richard N. Piland.)

This c. 1910 photograph shows the large bathhouse that opened in 1893 and a short bridge leading to a waterslide running into the lake. The large two-story building had a ladies dressing room on the second floor and men's changing rooms on the ground level. A vine-covered tunnel led to the beach. Park patrons could rent bathing suits for a small fee. Professional instructors provided swimming lessons free of charge to anyone needing them. (Al Carlisle.)

Many Kansas City area groups and organizations held annual picnics at Fairmount Park. Some of the largest functions involved more than 30,000 people and were sponsored by the Kansas City Street Railway Company, the Grocer's Association, Loose-Wiles Biscuit Company, and Montgomery Ward. The Cosmopolitan Club, a short-lived group of businessmen and citizens that grew to become the Independence Chamber of Commerce, poses for this photograph in 1919. (Harry S. Truman Library.)

This 1906 photograph shows the interior of the park's pavilion, which was located close to the Fairmount Hotel that was built in 1896. The pavilion was a multipurpose facility used for private functions with seating for several hundred people, free concerts for children, dances, and some of the activities during Chautauqua meetings held in the park. (Library of Congress, Prints and Photographs Division.)

Concerts, especially those performed by military bands, were very popular with the park's patrons. The small bandstand that existed when the park first opened was replaced in 1898 with the much larger one seen in this 1907 photograph. It was 60 feet wide and shaped like a small amphitheater, which provided excellent acoustics. Nearly 2,000 people could occupy bench seating for concerts, which were given at least once every day and always twice on Sundays. (Library of Congress, Prints and Photographs Division.)

The park closed after the 1901 season and remained idle until it reopened in May 1905, several months after the Standard Oil refinery began producing kerosene. Many top-level vaudeville acts, plays, and movies were presented at the park's auditorium. New rides such as this Figure 8 roller coaster were added to the park in 1906. The coaster rises 60 feet above the park and makes a figure-eight route around the park with people riding in cushioned leather seats. (Leigh Ann Little.)

As early as 1897, the park had a small zoo that was a special attraction for children. Inside were bears, a deer-petting pen, and several Shetland ponies for youngsters to ride. The 4:00 p.m. feeding time for the animals might have been a special treat for children. One of the park's three roller coasters can be seen in this photograph above and beyond the zoo enclosure.

This photograph taken in 1921 shows one of the arcade-type attractions that were popular at the park. The Fun House seen here was one of many new features meant to entertain park patrons. Over the years, park management added attractions such as the Jack Rabbit figure-eight ride, Captive Airplane, Double Whirl, and the Big Dipper, a 5,375-foot-long roller coaster going faster than 60 miles per hour with a dozen drops up to 86 feet.

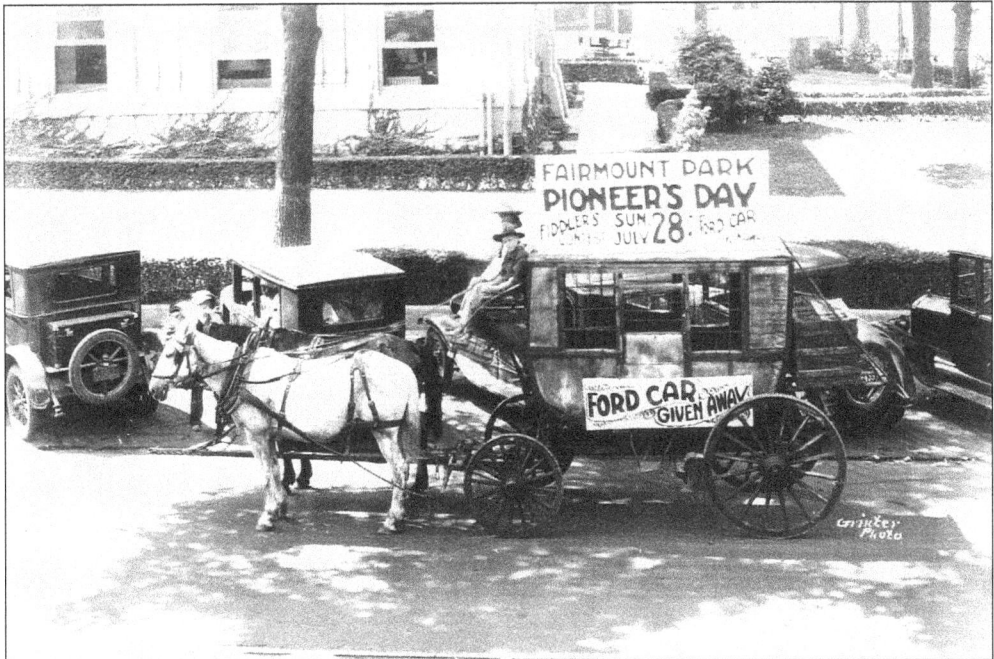

Automobiles were allowed on park grounds beginning in 1913. Parking was free, but passengers paid 10¢ each to enter the park. A new ride in 1922 was the Auto Raceway, featuring 12 gasoline-powered midget cars patrons could drive on a racetrack. In keeping with the car theme, the park staged periodic automobile giveaways, such as the one advertised here to promote the park. The efforts did not succeed. Fairmount Park closed in 1935.

In February 1904, an agent secretly acting on behalf of the Standard Oil Company of Indiana bought 30 acres of land from William Mallinson and 20 acres each from George Collins and Hugh McElroy for a refinery. J. E. Evans (left), the refinery's first superintendent, managed initial construction of the facility including development of the tank farm, blacksmith and machine shops, pipe shop, railroad yard, fire department, and water works. His work to establish the refinery led residents to name Evans Street in his honor. George H. Moffett (right) was also involved in the refinery's construction and served as the plant's second superintendent from 1908 to 1939.

By early summer 1904, substantial progress in the construction of the refinery had been made as recorded in this photograph. Nearly 700 men worked 10-hour days, six days a week to build the facility. Wages ranged from 17.5¢ per hour for common laborers to 62.5¢ per hour for masons. The workforce included at least 235 boilermakers, 180 pipe shop men, 29 masons, 55 carpenters, two blacksmiths, three machine shop staff, 10 watchmen, 14 office workers, two messenger boys, four water boys, and more than 150 laborers.

On September 26, the pipeline connecting the refinery to the company's Kansas oil fields was complete, and the refinery produced its first shipment of kerosene on October 24. Men such as the workers seen in this photograph, many of whom came from Whiting, Indiana, were among the first Standard Oil employees in Sugar Creek. These employees are, from left to right, (first row) Raymond Oakley, J. A. Hininger, Robert C. Wetmore, J. E. Evans, G. H. Moffett, W. B. Basinger, W. P. Stenhouse, Victor C. Anderson, and Frank Gainor; (center) George E. Swan; (second row) Byas Harris, G. W. Thompson, J. E. Howell, W. B. Jennings, B. F. Roach, George Killian, and Harry Boger.

This building was the first headquarters and laboratory of the refinery. It was built in 1904 and located on Standard Street. It would be remodeled and expanded over the years until a new research and engineering office building was constructed on Kentucky Road in the 1950s.

The Sugar Creek Townsite Company was incorporated on March 24, 1904, with the purpose of acquiring, developing, and selling real estate that surrounded the refinery site. The 200 shares of capital stock in the company sold for $50 each and raised $10,000. Ten men purchased all the available stock and borrowed additional funds to finance the company's operations. The six shareholders who bought 10 shares each were Kit Colyer and J. L. Phelps of Independence and John M. Steele, Henry C. Brent, E. F. McElroy, and E. F. Edgecomb of Kansas City. C. C. Craver of Kansas City and W. L. Bryant of Independence purchased 20 shares each, and Albert M. Ott acquired 30 shares. The largest shareholder was T. T. Crittenden Jr., who owned 70 shares. Crittenden, seen in this 1908 photograph when he was mayor of Kansas City, was the son of Missouri governor T. T. Crittenden Sr., who issued the $10,000 reward that led to the death of outlaw Jesse James. (Richard N. Piland.)

Col. N. P. Simonds bought 32 acres of land in the Sugar Creek area in 1895. After the refinery began, he built homes on the property to be sold to Standard Oil employees. This image shows early construction on Cowan Avenue, named for W. P. Cowan, the Standard Oil director who oversaw construction of the Whiting, Indiana, refinery. In 1926, the city renamed the street Claremont Avenue.

A detail from the *1904 Plat Book for Jackson County* shows major features of the Sugar Creek area. At the top are the Missouri River and main line of the Atchison, Topeka and Santa Fe Railway. The refinery is surrounded by land owned by G. R. Collins, D. E. Larkin, N. P. Simonds, A. B. Crawford, and H. L. McElroy. Sugar Creek Townsite occupies the center, and Fairmount Park is in the lower left area. (Richard N. Piland.)

23

The Standard Warehouse feed store was located on the west side of Fairmount Avenue near Kentucky Avenue when this 1908 photograph was taken. The store provided hay, seed, coal, and other products for area farmers and residents. The warehouse's employees and the customers driving the two horse-drawn wagons are unknown. A fire destroyed the business sometime around 1910.

Cal Pendleton (left) and John Ford were two of the local farmers who tilled the rich agricultural area around Sugar Creek. The two men are seen in this 1902 photograph with a wagon full of produce in a small cornfield located in the Missouri River bottoms.

The west side of Fairmount Avenue near the Chicago Street intersection is seen in this photograph dating from 1908. The post office had a wall-mounted telephone and shared the building with a laundry. Businesses in the adjacent building included a barbershop, public bath, and at least one other store. The boy sitting on the horse is seven-year-old Frank Larkin Jr. Larkin's family sold the farm they bought in the 1880s to Standard Oil in 1917 for one of the refinery's expansions.

This 1912 photograph was taken outside a general store and saloon on Fairmount Avenue. The customary mode of transportation for Sugar Creek area residents remained wagons powered by horses. The men are, from left to right, Alvis Smith, Matt Kobe, Bob Allen, and William Mallinson.

From the start, the general appearance of Sugar Creek was much the same as any other small Midwestern town. Most of the public's business is conducted on one main thoroughfare. For Sugar Creek, the major street was Fairmount Avenue, seen here as it was around 1914 or 1915 looking south from Evans Street. Nearly all of the businesses serving the needs of residents were located on this unpaved road. Stores along the street included a laundry, bakery, pool hall, barbershop, dry cleaner, hardware store, restaurant, bank, saloon, hotel, confectionery, feed store, post office, blacksmith, two grocery stores, and two shoe shops. (Laurel Ann Bonine.)

Two

SERVING THE COMMUNITY

Sugar Creek was essentially an agricultural area until construction of the Standard Oil refinery was started in 1904. The company brought a number of employees from its refinery in Whiting, Indiana, and hired local people to build the plant and begin production. Residential construction centered on the land around the refinery and Col. N. P. Simonds, a Kansas City grain dealer, built the area's first homes near the plant. Since there was no municipal government, residents depended on the refinery to provide water, fire protection, and other essential services. Law enforcement was administered by the Jackson County sheriff.

In nearly all respects, the Jackson County Court was the area's government until Sugar Creek was given city status on November 15, 1920. The court appointed the city's first group of officials. From that date, the town's business was determined by an elected mayor and board of aldermen. City status was primarily the result of the work done by the Sugar Creek Improvement Association, a group of businessmen and residents formed after World War I.

In 1921, the town's residents passed bond issues to build sanitary sewers and a water distribution system, and in 1925 they approved money for a new city hall building. Area voters also passed a bond issue to resurface Fairmount Avenue in 1925. Before Sugar Creek had received city status, voters passed bonds to build the Riverview School and its expansion and classroom additions. Over the years, the city's residents would continue to support bond issues for street improvements, sewers, park land acquisition and, in the 1960s, new buildings including a new city hall, a new fire and police building, and a new sewage disposal plant.

A volunteer fire department was established in the early 1920s, but it was ill equipped to deal with fires since it only had two hose carts pulled by cars or men until the city bought its first fire truck in 1925. A second fire truck was acquired in 1928. For many years, firefighting was done by a staff of only three to five men along with volunteers and fire departments from the refinery and nearby communities.

Sugar Creek law enforcement was vested in a town marshal who was elected by popular vote and served as the chief of police. The town had only one police cruiser for many years and, as late as 1964, had a police department of three officers and only two vehicles.

Garnett Lee Pittillo was a boilermaker at the Standard Oil refinery when he enlisted in the army to serve during World War I. Private Pittillo died on October 4, 1918, during fighting in Nevers, France, just five weeks before the end of the war. He was the third and last Sugar Creek man to be killed during the war. Other local soldiers killed in the fighting were Pvt. George Beal on July 19, 1918, and Pvt. R. K. Mayfield on September 28, 1918.

Carl Smee was one of the Sugar Creek men who fought for his country during World War I. He and his wife posed for this image taken around 1919. The Smees were active participants in the early life of the city. After the war, Smee served as the town's first postmaster and Mrs. Smee, among other things, was the president of the Sugar Creek Parent-Teacher Association during 1926 and 1927.

The first mayor of Sugar Creek was H. R. Boehmer, who was appointed to the position by the Jackson County Court when the city was incorporated in November 1920. The next year, Boehmer was elected mayor by popular vote and served in the position until 1929. During his years in office, he also worked as the superintendent of the Standard Oil refinery. After being mayor, Boehmer served on the Sugar Creek Board of Education for nine years.

Before 1925, the Sugar Creek City Council met in the schoolhouse until offices were rented in a store on the corner of Fairmount Avenue and Chicago Street and then in the Slyman Building. Voters, by a vote of 150 to 50, approved a $16,000 bond to pave Fairmount Avenue and a second bond of $10,000 to build a city hall. The new city hall seen in this photograph was officially occupied on April 16, 1926.

Sugar Creek's streets were mainly hard-packed dirt or macadamized roads during the 1900s and 1910s. Around 1920, the intersection of Kentucky and Fairmount Avenues, seen above, was little more than a meeting of two dirt roads. The railroad crossing on Kentucky Avenue at the center of the image is where the Maywood and Sugar Creek Railroad carried petroleum tank cars south out of the refinery to Kansas City and other markets. Streets leading off to the left would take traffic into Fairmount Park. The c. 1920 photograph below shows Fairmount Avenue south from Elizabeth Street. The refinery can be seen to the right. The one-lane bridge the car is crossing spans Sugar Creek, the stream that gave the community its name. (Below, Laurel Ann Bonine.)

Prior to the city's formation in 1920, fire departments in nearby communities or at the Standard Oil refinery would be called to extinguish fires in Sugar Creek. An explosion of an oil lamp in Rodman's saloon caused a fire that destroyed the building and an adjacent pool hall in 1908. Even though the refinery's firemen responded, the loss of the two structures was estimated at about $7,000. This March 1925 receipt shows that Sugar Creek paid the Fairmount Fire Department $25 for responding to a fire in the city.

During the early 1920s, the city government set out to solve problems facing the community. Contracts for electrical power, water supply, sanitation facilities, and sewers were approved. The town's first water tower was erected in the southeast part of the city in 1923. The 50,000-gallon capacity tower seen here would serve the city well until it was torn down in March 1966.

The photograph above, taken at the rear of city hall in 1928, shows one of the two original hose carts city officials purchased in 1924 and the town's first two fire engines: the left one bought in 1925 and the right one bought in 1928. Below, members of Sugar Creek's volunteer fire department stand next to the city's second fire truck that had been purchased for $7,050 in January 1928. The men dressed in their firefighting gear are, from left to right, Chief Frank Diesko, Mike Kobe, Ballard Ladel, Joe Povalich, Mac McGriffen, and Clifford Howard. Most of the volunteers also worked at the Standard Oil refinery and several served the city in other capacities.

These men were the elected leadership that administered the city during the early years of the Great Depression. From left to right are aldermen Glenn Buckley and Perry McAvoy, Mayor John W. Kelly, and aldermen Fred Dickey and James Van Winkle. Kelly was the town's second mayor and served six terms from 1929 to 1941.

Sugar Creek had a post office by 1904. In early years, it was located on Elizabeth Street near the refinery, then it shared space with several different businesses before moving to the State Bank Building at the corner of Chicago Street and Fairmount Avenue. By 1938, it had relocated to this building at 412 Sterling Avenue. Another move was made in 1952 to 106 Sterling Avenue, where the post office would remain until 1975. (Laurel Ann Bonine.)

The U.S. Census for 1940 counted 1,638 residents living in Sugar Creek. Selective Service registration numbered 191 men that year, and many more men and women entered the military over the next five years to serve during World War II. The billboard seen in this photograph was erected on the city hall lawn in 1942. It lists an honor roll of 282 men and women from Sugar Creek in service to the country. Eleven of the men listed died during the fighting. The names Cecil D. Sooter, Kenneth McGaw, Dean Darby, Michael Dumsky, Frank Clemens, Andrew Paloney, Douglas M. Fulkerson, Joseph Bruson, Eldon E. Means, Claude Danforth, and Ross Buckley would be placed on the monument in the town's Memorial Park to honor their sacrifices.

Several Sugar Creek men returning from military service during World War II gather outside the Sugar Creek Pharmacy at 514 Sterling Avenue in this 1946 photograph. The happy veterans facing the camera are, from left to right, George Balko, Larry Kinney, Steve Kobe, George Payur, John Halastic, unknown, John Kimak, and John Mikulich.

Problems related to public water supply and sanitary sewers were among the first concerns addressed by the first Sugar Creek City Council. In 1921, a $25,000 bond issue for city sewers was approved by voters. Construction of the Inter-City sewer line began in 1937. In this 1949 image, two young boys watch a crew of four men prepare to install sewer pipes north from Kentucky Avenue along Carlisle Street.

In 1950, Sugar Creek purchased a new American La France fire engine for $15,434 to replace the old 1927 model that had served the city for years. The three firemen standing by the new truck are, from left to right, Bill Kluska, Emil Dykal, and fire chief Frank Kluska. The building in the background is the Sugar Creek Post Office, located on Sterling Avenue opposite city hall.

Sugar Creek police chief Mitchell Butkovich stands next to the department's only police cruiser in this photograph taken in front of City Hall in 1955. Butkovich served in the position for less than one year. He was replaced by Mike D. Onka, who was the town's chief of police until his death in 1968.

36

Mike D. Onka became Sugar Creek's police chief on April 1, 1955. During the late 1950s, the department consisted of three officers. Onka and Sgt. Clyde Hatfield handled all police activity during weekdays, while officer "Blackie" Rozgay worked weekends. Chief Onka would serve the city until he was killed in the line of duty while answering an armed robbery call on February 5, 1968.

Sugar Creek first organized a civil defense program in 1944 when W. G. Linnell was named the first director of the department. By 1959, the Civil Defense Unit included 60 block wardens, four block captains, 10 auxiliary firemen, 10 auxiliary policemen, and three vehicles. The city stored emergency supplies in the old Sugar Creek School building. In this 1962 photograph, civil defense leader Michael J. Marek (left) checks the local inventory of supplies with two unidentified men.

In 1962, voters passed bonds to build two new city buildings. One bond funded the construction of a new $190,000 city hall located at the southeast corner of Sterling and Kentucky Avenues. Facilities in the two-story, 5,000-square-foot center (above) included city council chambers, a conference room, small kitchen, vault, storage room, offices for the mayor and city officials, and a room for the dental clinic. A separate $120,000 bond paid for the new police and fire building (below). This two-story building was constructed on the site of the original city hall that had served the community since 1925. The new facility had room for offices, sleeping quarters, a kitchen, two fire engines, and two cars on the lower level. Additional offices for the city marshal, police department, civil defense director, a small courtroom and judge's office, and two detention cells were on the upper floor.

Graduates of the Sugar Creek Police Department's first police academy posed for this graduation class portrait in 1966. The academy was sponsored by Jackson County sheriff Arvid Owsley, and most of the classes were taught by special agents of the Kansas City field office of the FBI. The officers, from left to right, are (first row) Tony Novak, Herb Soule, Ralph Kelsey, Rocky Rowden, Anthony Bokarae, and police judge Virgil Lynch; (second row) Eddie Collins, George Payur, Glenn Newton, chief of police Mike Onka, Andy Anderson, and Earle Conner.

The Sugar Creek mayor and board of aldermen posed for this 1965 photograph in council chambers at the new city hall that had opened in 1963. The community's leadership includes, from left to right, city clerk John W. Gavin, aldermen Anthony Jasso and Steve Salva, Mayor R. J. Roper, and aldermen Ernie Wells and Charley Dumsky.

Officials from several jurisdictions in Jackson County were at Marshal Mike D. Onka's funeral in 1968. Above are, from left to right, (first row) acting Sugar Creek police chief William C. Morton, Independence police chief George Owens, and Robert Rhinehart; (second row) John Lucas (partially hidden), Rondell Stewart, and John Hix; to the far left are Steve Visnish and Fred Coats (partially hidden); court clerk Ray Sims stands near the curtain in the center. Below are members of the Sugar Creek Police Department who attended the funeral. They are, from left to right, George Payur, Joe Pugh (partially hidden), Chuck Main, Ralph Anderson, Ralph Kelsey, Bob Clark, and Bob Tally.

Voters first elected Irene B. Niederland to be city collector in 1942 when she was 32 years old. She was reelected to the position several times and served as collector for the city for more than 30 years. This photograph was taken sometime in the late 1970s and shows her at her desk in city hall.

Virgil Lynch (left) and H. R. Simms admire the Tulip Flag growing on the lawn of the Sugar Creek City Hall. The floral plot was created as part of the town's observance of the American bicentennial in 1976.

Rudy J. Roper retired after 40 years as mayor of Sugar Creek in 1981. He was only the third person to serve in the position. Roper and city clerk Veronica Powell hold the proclamation signed by Gov. Christopher Bond naming April 1, 1981, as "Rudy Roper Day" in the state of Missouri.

Herb Soule joined the Sugar Creek Police Department as a patrolman in 1966 before being called to serve in the U.S. Army Criminal Investigative Division in Vietnam. He returned to the local police department in 1969 and was promoted to sergeant in 1977 and captain in 1995. Sugar Creek voters elected him to be city marshal and chief of police in 2001. Soule was reelected by popular vote in 2005 and 2009.

Three

BUSINESS AND INDUSTRY

The earliest businesses in and around the Sugar Creek area catered to the needs of local farmers and landowners. Many residents traveled to nearby Independence or Kansas City to get the goods they needed. Grain seed, animal feed, coal, lumber, and all sorts of other products required for farming were within a few miles. There were several family farms, such as the ones owned by James Mallinson, who came to the county in 1859; J. D. Cusenberry, who farmed and bred horses; and D. E. Larkin, who established a leading potato farm.

With the arrival of the Standard Oil refinery in 1904, however, commercial development in Sugar Creek began. The first businesses in Sugar Creek were those that served the primary needs of the people who had come to build the refinery. Several grocery and dry goods stores opened to provide food to residents. Other merchants supplied customers with feed and coal, lumber and building supplies, and housing. Mike Onka, one of the first to establish a grocery in town, also operated a boardinghouse for refinery employees. Grocery stores were also started by George Mossie, Harry Kamensky, and J. F. McMains.

Sugar Creek grew much like most small towns in the Midwest. Many of the community's businesses were located on one main street, Fairmount Avenue. In the early days, there were several saloons, restaurants, pool halls, bathhouses, a bank, and shops—all housed in wooden buildings. Nearby, on the southern side of the area, was Fairmount Park and resort, another important business.

As the refinery grew, so did the economic fortunes of the town. Two railroads served the community. The Atchison, Topeka and Santa Fe Railway began service between Kansas City and Chicago in 1888 and built a Sugar Creek station in 1904. The Maywood and Sugar Creek Railroad, a 2-mile-long railway built to serve the refinery, also started in 1904. It became part of the Kansas City Southern Railway, which grew from a railroad started by Arthur Stillwell, the man who also developed Fairmount Park.

Businesses in Sugar Creek evolved to include gasoline stations, pharmacies, appliance stores, furniture stores, auto-repair shops, beauty and barbershops, taverns, liquor stores, restaurants, beer distributors, and trucking companies. The community had a solid economic base, anchored by the Standard Oil refinery and the addition through annexations of companies such as the Missouri Portland Cement Company.

The Standard Feed Store warehouse, located at the corner of Fairmount and Kentucky Avenues, provided area farmers and landowners with the seed, feed, and coal they needed for their livestock and homes during the early 1900s. The men standing on the loading dock at the store are, from left to right, owner R. Rudge, Sid Buford, Bud Buford, Bus Pittillo, and King Mayfield.

This undated photograph shows the Larkin Brothers at work packing some of their crop of potatoes at their farm in the Missouri River bottoms near Cement City. Larkin family members were longtime residents of the area and owned 80 acres of land east of the town in 1904. In 1913, Benjamin Franklin Larkin traveled to lobby Missouri governor Eliot Major to allow Standard Oil to remain in the state. Larkin served as president of the Jackson County Potato Growers Association in the 1940s.

George M. Rodman (right), one of the first saloon operators in Sugar Creek, stands outside his bar with patron John Henderson Thatch. His first saloon and an adjacent billiards parlor were destroyed by fire after an oil lamp exploded in the bar in 1908. Even though the refinery fire department fought the blaze, the loss was estimated at $7,000. Rodman soon opened another saloon and became a vigorous foe of the anti-saloon movement in Jackson County.

The town's first post office began operations on Elizabeth Street in 1904. By 1913, it was housed at the back of the hardware store seen in this photograph. Postmaster Lemuel W. Ballinger and an unidentified child are seen outside the post office windows. Ballinger was also an inventor who held a patent for an oil burner for cook and heating stoves that he sold in his store. Within three years, the post office moved to a new location in the new State Bank Building.

In 1868, James Mallinson purchased his original family farm, which was divided among his heirs after his death in 1887. Some land was sold to Standard Oil for the refinery and some kept for a dairy farm started by Roy and John Mallinson, two of James's grandsons. The photograph above shows some of the Mallinson dairy herd watched by two unidentified milkers. The short building behind the barn is a blacksmith shop. The house at the top includes the original log cabin built on the property in 1867. Below, Roy Mallinson sits behind the wheel of the dairy's delivery truck, a 1913 Vim model purchased in 1915. This picture was taken in Kansas City, when Mallinson was parked opposite the Verne O. Williams Photography Studio.

The State Bank of Sugar Creek was chartered on June 10, 1914, and capitalized at $10,000. On January 9, 1920, the capitalized stock was increased to $20,000. The bank, seen here in a photograph taken in 1914 or 1915, occupies the left half of the building, and a bakery sold goods from the right half. The structure at the far left is the Underwood Barber Shop. (Laurel Ann Bonine.)

The interior of the State Bank of Sugar Creek was quite Spartan when this photograph was taken in 1915: two teller windows, one window for the cashier, and three spittoons. The bank moved to a new building in 1916. After the bank vacated the building, Mike Bines used it as a hotel between 1916 and 1920. In later years, the Manners Taxidermy Shop was located here from 1948 through the 1970s, and Tom Jerry's Sterling Café did business here from 1952 to 1968 before moving to the Fairmount business district.

This two-story brick structure was built at Chicago Street and Fairmount Avenue for the State Bank of Sugar Creek in 1915. The bank fell victim to the Depression and closed on January 27, 1934. In March 1939, the Missouri Department of Finance returned almost $111,000 to depositors.

In 1926, the High Grade Food Store took over the portion of the State Bank Building that had been occupied by the post office. Stephen W. Loksik owned the grocery store until he sold his business to Stanley J. Bukaty in 1939. By 1942, Bukaty sold the store to Mike D. Onka, who would operate a grocery and meat market there until the 1960s.

James F. McMains opened his grocery store at the corner of Fairmount Avenue and Chicago Street in 1905. He was president of the community's first board of education and was in office when area voters passed a bond issue to build the Riverview School in 1906. McMains is giving a package to an unidentified customer while employee Bob Allen stands under a Mica Axle Grease advertisement.

As early as 1906, the Badger Lumber Company operated the fenced-in lumberyard and coal shed at the corner of Fairmount and Kentucky Avenues seen to the left in this photograph. Badger replaced the Bowman-Hicks lumber company, which had been ousted from the state after being convicted of price fixing and limiting the amount of yellow pine manufactured in Missouri. After the lumberyard closed in 1938, R. J. Roper acquired the property and constructed a new building on the site.

Harry Kamensky opened a dry goods store in 1904 and expanded his products to include meats in 1906. Kamensky's United Merchandise Company later moved to a new brick building on Fairmount Avenue (above); Harry stands directly in front of the store's door at left. The business in the right half of the building is a clothing store operated by the unidentified man in front. During the Depression, Kamensky extended credit on faith to many unemployed Sugar Creek residents. The people in the store (below) are, from left to right, Harry Kamensky, Wallace Crouch, John Beal, Nick O'Renick, George Vida, Helen Kobe, and Ann O'Renick. (Above, Laurel Ann Bonine.)

Wallace Crouch, the butcher at Kamensky's grocery, is behind the steering wheel of the store's truck in this photograph taken sometime between 1938 and 1940. The truck and the unidentified young man are in front of the United Merchandise store located at 605 North Sterling. Kamensky sold the store to Stanley J. Bukaty in 1945. (Laurel Ann Bonine.)

Ellis Cairns operated a jitney service between Sugar Creek and Independence from 1937 to 1946. Cairns's taxis took people to Independence where they could catch a streetcar to Kansas City. The men standing next to the company's school bus and fleet of four taxis are, from left to right, Ellis Cairns, Nick Stanley, Mike Onka, Mike Kimak, and John Kimak.

Roy Fulkerson's Service Garage was located on Fairmount Avenue immediately north of city hall and the fire station during the 1920s and 1930s. The filling station sold Red Crown and White Crown gasoline and a variety of other Standard Oil products, as well as Goodyear tires, and promised 24-hour service. The garage remained open until the Kaw Transport Company acquired the location in 1942. The 13 men in this photograph taken before 1937 are, from left to right, (seated) John Kroll, Steve Kobe and Sherman Kamensky; (first row) unknown, Steve Benkovich, John Pavola, unknown, Louie Fries, unknown, Joe Topi, and Harry Lee; (second row) Mate Butkovich and unknown. The building beyond the garage had been used by Mike Juricak for his Do Drop Inn Tavern, R. K. Shoemaker for the *Jackson County Herald* newspaper, and for Reorganized Church of Jesus Christ of Latter Day Saints (RLDS) church services. The next building was the R. O. Snyder Feed Store, and the brick building with the awning in the distance is the Kamensky grocery store.

Mike and Sophia Onka opened one of the first grocery stores in Sugar Creek on Evans Avenue in 1904. Their son Mike D. Onka operated this grocery store in the same building on Sterling Avenue that had held the Stephen Loksik and Stanley Bukaty grocery stores in earlier years. Pictured from left to right in this 1942 photograph are Irene Neiderland, Mike D. Onka, John Onka, John Onka, Jr., ? Patrick, Ed Maglich, and John Kunca.

Stephen A. Petrechko operated a popular barbeque restaurant and tavern on the southwest corner of Fairmount and Evans Avenues from the 1920s until the mid-1940s. Petrechko (right) stands with an unidentified employee outside the business in this photograph taken in the early 1920s. One of the refinery's thermal stills towers above the back of the restaurant. In later years, another tavern would be operated by Nick Roper at this location.

Andy Manners opened his taxidermy and sports shop at 713 North Sterling Avenue in 1946 and remained in business at the location until the 1970s. Earlier occupants of the building had included the State Bank of Sugar Creek, Sugar Creek Church of God, and Carr's Second Hand Furniture Store. In this image, Manners (left) examines a pelt that Grant Morgan brought to the store.

The Standard Furniture Company was begun by R. L. Bennett before 1923 as a vendor of new and secondhand goods. By 1940, the store, which was at the intersection of Norledge and Sterling Avenues, added hardware items to its inventory. This 1947 photograph was taken after the store had relocated to the corner of Chicago Street and Sterling Avenue. Outside the store are, from left to right, (first row) Andrew Petrechko Jr.; (second row) Mary Zevecke, Eleanor Petrechko, Denise Petrechko, and Susie Zevecke.

This photograph shows the businesses that were operating in the new Roper Building on the northwest corner of Kentucky and Sterling Avenues in 1941. The largest part of the building is occupied by the Standard Oil service station. The two stores to the right are a small furniture and hardware store owned by Pete Saxton and Lewis Pierce's Standard Pharmacy. Rudy Roper operated his beer distributing business out of the lower level at the rear of the building.

The Kansas City Portland Cement Company began operations in 1906 when a group of investors purchased 75 acres of riverfront land east of Sugar Creek and the Standard Oil refinery. Within one year, more than 300 people worked at the plant. The only way to get to the cement plant was through Sugar Creek. By 1915, a jitney service between the Independence town square and Cement City was shuttling workers on a very bone-jarring ride over the narrow rock road to the factory. (Laurel Ann Bonine.)

The nearby Portland Cement plant was the third to begin production in Missouri. The first two plants were started in 1902 in St. Louis and in 1903 in Hannibal. By 1925, the company's workers had dug more than 5 miles of tunnels into the hillside above the Missouri River and turned over three million tons of Pennsylvanian limestone and shale into powder to make concrete. This undated photograph shows the entrances of the first set of tunnels into the mine.

The cement plant's facilities included a variety of rock crushers, several mills, kilns, dryers, rolling cylinders, storage silos, cement tanks, a machine shop, and offices. This photograph from the 1930s shows some of the company's fleet of trucks loaded with rocks ready for crushing to make the base powder for cement. A portion of one of the tunnel entrances can be seen at the extreme right side of the photograph.

56

A 1926 view of the Portland cement plant (above) is looking east down the Atchison, Topeka and Santa Fe double mainline track from the Sugar Creek side. The tall structure in the right foreground is part of the rock crusher operation. The closest conveyer over the tracks connects the plant's kiln building to the shed over a coal dump and elevator. The distant conveyer connects the cement stock house with the packing and shipping house. Over the years, the plant expanded with changes in technology and market demands. An aerial view (below), taken in 1940, shows the Missouri River in the lower right, Cement City Road along the riverbank, and the old Wayne City–River Road on the bluff overlooking the plant. In 1964, the entire area became part of Sugar Creek when the city annexed about 2,300 acres. (Above, Richard N. Piland.)

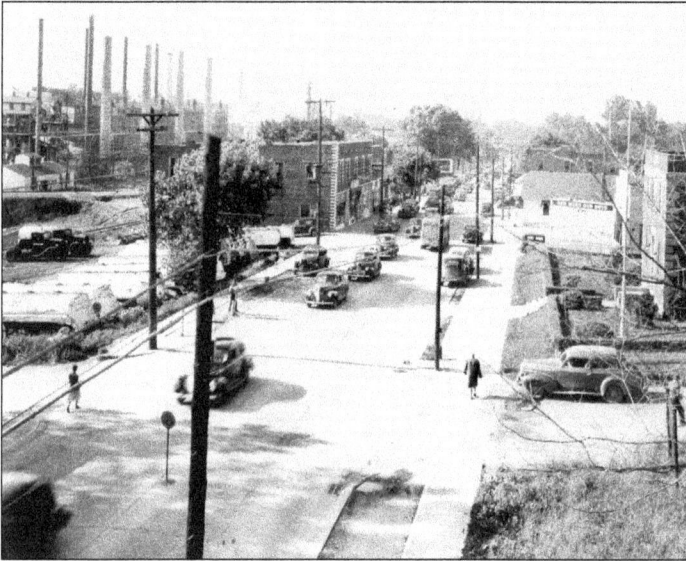

Sterling Avenue bustled with activity when this photograph was taken in May 1946. City Hall with the "God Bless Our Boys" billboard on the lawn, listing the names of the men and women serving during World War II, is on the right. The building to the left center is Slyman's Hall, which housed Sullivan's Sugar Creek Pharmacy and Cliff's Place Restaurant. Towering over the scene are the constant reminders of the Standard Oil refinery.

Nick Roper opened his tavern in 1946 in the same building that previously had been used for Steve Petrechko's barbeque and tavern. The small, white frame building on the southwest corner of Sterling and Evans Avenues was renamed the Sugar Inn in 1969. Given the tavern's location, many of Roper's customers worked at the refinery. The structure to the left of the tavern is the City Transit Garage. (Laurel Ann Bonine.)

This photograph, taken sometime between 1948 and 1950, shows Alma Manners standing behind the counter of the taxidermy and tannery shop operated by her husband, Andy. Alma worked part-time in the shop and also served the community by hauling the mail during the 1940s.

Kaw Transport opened temporary offices in Sugar Creek in 1942. This c. 1950 photograph shows several company petroleum tankers parked in the company's lot directly across from city hall. Kaw Transport was one of the dominant haulers of the gasoline refined at Standard Oil refinery. The building to the right center in the picture is a sidewall of Slyman Hall.

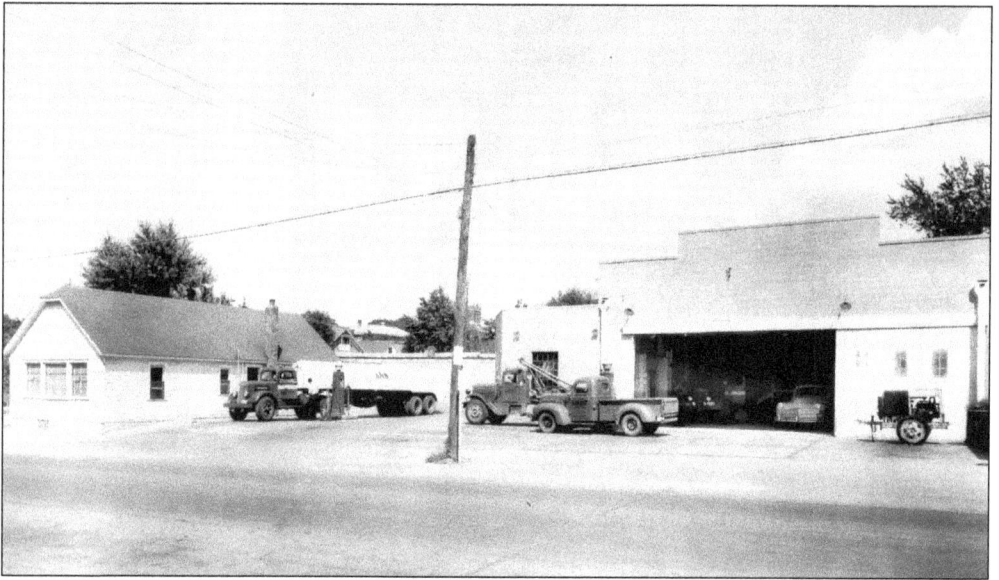

Kaw Transport Company acquired the Fulkerson garage in 1942 and an adjacent building in 1944 when the company moved its main office to Sugar Creek. Kaw's office, seen to the left of the maintenance shop, was in a remodeled building that previously had been home to the town's weekly newspaper, a tavern, and church services. The company relocated its office to the corner of Sterling Avenue and Chicago Street in 1959 and then closed its Sugar Creek office in 1968.

One of the Kaw Transport Company's tank trucks hauls a load of gasoline out of the refinery in this photograph dating from the mid-1950s. Refined products produced in Sugar Creek were shipped in either tanker trucks like this one or in railroad tank cars by the Atchison, Topeka and Santa Fe or Kansas City Southern Railroads. (Jim Steele.)

Mayor Rudy Roper stands in the doorway of a Kansas City Public Service bus that provided a link between Sugar Creek and Fairmount during the 1950s. The other men taking the bus for a lunch at Jerry's Café in Fairmount are, from left to right, Pete Saxton, Concie O'Connell, Steve Salva, John W. Gavin, C. W. McKaughan, D. B. Eyer (bus company president), Anthony Jasso, and W. G. Linnell.

Mayor Rudy Roper stands on his company's entry in Sugar Creek's 1959 Independence Day Parade. The float, in part, celebrated the 20th anniversary of his beer distribution company. The happy riders on the float are, from left to right, Pat Cholak, Patricia Beal, Carole Roper, and Rudy Roper.

Mattie's Drive-In Restaurant was a very popular place for area residents, especially the town's teenagers, after it opened in 1960. The people at the counter are, from left to right, Bob Weaver, unknown, Jean Christensen, Linda Sapp, Tootie Butkovich, and Mate Butkovich. The building is now the home of the Sugar Creek Historical Center and the Friends of Sugar Creek. (Tootie Butkovich.)

The Atchison, Topeka and Santa Fe Railway Company first laid a main line track through Sugar Creek in November 1887 and began passenger service between Kansas City and Chicago in 1888. The first Sugar Creek depot opened in 1904, shortly after Standard Oil began production and the town site had been established. This late 1960s photograph shows the town's depot facing the Santa Fe double main line and the spur leading from the refinery passing behind the station.

Four

BUILDING SOUND MINDS

Prior to 1906, the only formal education for children available in the Sugar Creek area was the classes taught in nearby private subscription schools in Independence or at various locations in the community. After the Sugar Creek Townsite Company was formed in 1904, it platted 1 acre for a school. Local residents unanimously voted for a $33,000 bond issue to build a four-room brick schoolhouse on that land.

The Riverview School, built near the corner of Chicago and Cowan Streets, was an elementary school serving the children of the area. The Standard Oil refinery provided water to the school by running a small pipeline to the building. Three girls were in the school's first graduation class in 1909. Voters passed a second bond issue in 1912 for $12,000 to add four classrooms, which were ready for students in 1914.

In 1921, the north building was constructed after a $50,000 bond was passed. The new structure included four additional classrooms and an auditorium. The name of the two-part complex was changed to Sugar Creek School. A parent-teacher organization was formed in 1920 with Alice Jones, a resident of the area since 1903, serving as the group's first president. Many of the people who served on the board of education were business leaders, Standard Oil managers, and community notables.

Plans for a gymnasium for the school were made as early as 1941, but construction was deferred because of World War II. In 1948, students and community members were able to enjoy the facility when it was completed.

The school district made substantial efforts to meet the needs of students. Because no high school was available in town, the board of education paid tuition and provided bus transportation for students to attend either Northeast High School in Kansas City or William Chrisman High School in Independence. The district also provided students with school supplies and a health clinic, including low-cost dental services for preschool children.

In 1955, Sugar Creek voters approved a plan to join the Kansas City (Missouri) School District. The community had passed a $620,000 bond for a new elementary school before the district was annexed, and the new building opened in 1956. Young students had a state-of-the art elementary school, and older students attended the brand new Van Horn High School.

The first school building in Sugar Creek was the Riverview School, built in 1906 at the corner of Chicago and Cowan Streets. Construction of the four-room brick school was made possible by a $33,000 bond issue that was passed by residents with a vote of 47 to 0. The members of the first school board were James F. McMains, J. F. Anderson, and James Burton. The school's first principal was Anna Collins.

Commencement exercises were held for the first class to graduate from Riverview School on June 17, 1909. The graduating class consisted of Etha Cramer, Lutie Cannon, and Rose Larkin; the class motto was "Not at the top, but still climbing." A program cover for the exercises is seen here. (Laurel Ann Bonine.)

Students in Miss Haynes's fourth- or fifth-grade class stand outside the Riverview School around 1910. Youngsters in the class are, from left to right, (first row) Joe Marsh, Geraldine Hackett, Mary Mallinson, Mary Burkhart, Jessie Hixson, Lancer Lee, unknown, Rose Dumsky, Lola Decker, Lillian Kamensky, Myrtle Decker, unknown, Vern Sutton, and Frank Larkin; (second row) unknown, Pearl Mallinson, Frances Foster, Mary Murray, Elizabeth Hink, unknown, and Virgie Pennington; (third row) unknown, Bruce Hixson, Elva Thatch, Leon Sutton, and Jarvis Mayfield.

In this c. 1910 photograph, 10 Sugar Creel School students are seen playing on the Atchison, Topeka and Santa Fe double main line north of the refinery. The youngsters, from front to back, are (left side) Fred Hink, Emma Murray, Warnie Hatten, Elizabeth Hink, and unknown; (right side) Ione Hackett, Lancer Lee, Mary Murray, Vern Sutton, and Shelton Huffman.

After the town's children graduated from the local grade school, they would attend Northeast High School in Kansas City. The Sugar Creek Board of Education paid tuition and provided free bus service. This image shows a busload of unidentified students sometime around 1925.

Students in the Riverview School's fourth-grade class in 1919 or 1920 are, from left to right, (first row) Myrtle Turner, teacher Miss Boutcher, and Mary Juricak; (second row) Theodore Carver, unknown, Ray Johnson, Ballard Todd, Frank Woolridge, Roy Johnson, Gordon Stoner, Sherman Kamensky, and Joe Lynn; (third row) Ruth Stinnett, Irene Lynch, Edna Spradley, Lena Evinger, Dan O'Connell, Lee Evinger, John Meyrnick, Francis Phillips, and John Onka.

The old Riverview School, which had been enlarged with four additional classrooms in 1913 after a $12,000 bond issue, makes up the right half of the school building in this image. On the left is the new Sugar Creek School, which added four more classrooms, a cafeteria, and an auditorium to meet student needs when it was completed in 1921. Students could attend eight grades in the building for many years, and when they reached high school age they were bused to either Northeast or Chrisman High Schools. Voters approved a $55,000 bond in 1941 to build a new gymnasium at the school, but construction was delayed until after World War II. The new facility was completed after the war and opened to the public during the winter of the 1948–1949 school year.

Sugar Creek resident Mary Rose Vukas is dressed for her graduation from St. Mary's Academy in Independence in this 1934 photograph. Mary later attended the Castor School of Cosmetology. She and her husband, John Rozgay, were actively involved in sponsoring and coaching youth baseball teams in the Sugar Creek and Fairmount areas.

The Sugar Creek School furnished books and school supplies free to many of its students. The district also provided health services, including a tonsil clinic and dental services for a modest fee of 25¢ per visit. By 1937, a clinic for preschool children was added to the health services. In this c. 1935 photograph, Dr. Albert V. Frisby (right) and nurse Olive Curry work with an unidentified patient at the dental clinic held in the Sugar Creek City Hall.

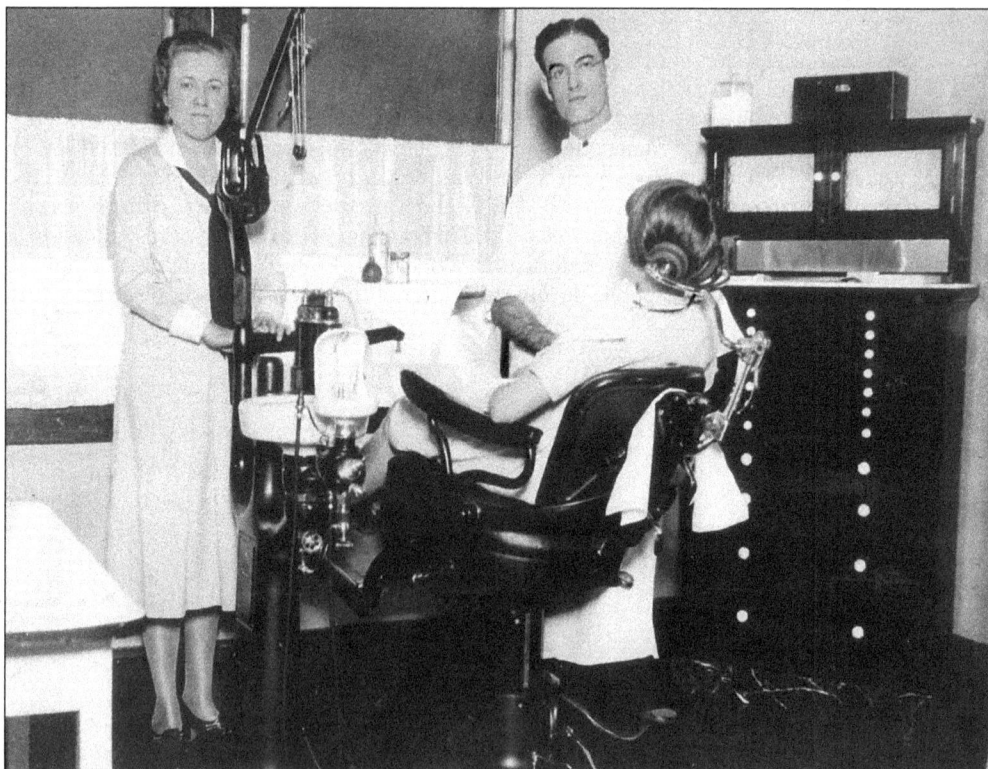

Twenty-five unidentified girls took part in a production of *The Princess Who Couldn't Dance* at the Sugar Creek School stage and auditorium during a Works Progress Administration recreation project in 1938. The program was staged by Margit Daghy, the tall woman behind the costumed girls. Several other government-sponsored Depression-era projects for Sugar Creek girls and boys were part of the National Youth Assistance program.

Iris Cairns stands at the door of the school bus she drove for her father's company, the Sugar Creek-Independence Jitney Company, in this late 1930s photograph. Cairns would take young Sugar Creek School students to the high school they attended and any other locations required by their teachers.

During the early 1940s, most of the teachers at Sugar Creek School were women. The school's faculty members seen in this photograph are, from left to right, (first row) Jim Sexton, Edith C. Pritchett, Ann Lowman, and Lola Stanley; (second row) Elsie Brune, Ella Penick, janitor Hugh Danforth, and Lillian Bales; (third row) Margaret Lee Surber, Mamie Moore, Nurse Swain, principal J. Raymond Guy, and Ethel Bayless.

At least 50 students took part in the spring operetta that was performed in the Sugar Creek School's auditorium in 1936. The auditorium seen in this photograph was in the portion of the north building addition that was constructed in 1921. During the 1930s and 1940s, the school became noted for its outstanding music program as well as for its health, athletic, and audio-visual programs.

Hugh Danforth, seen here in a May 1940 photograph, served as the Sugar Creek School's janitor and building maintenance person. He became the school's custodian in the 1920s after working at the refinery for several years and served in the school until the 1950s. During World War II, his son Claude was a prisoner of war who survived the Bataan Death March of 1942 but died on a prison ship headed for Japan in October 1944.

The girl's basketball team from the Sugar Creek School won the state tournament for small-town schools in 1944. The members of the championship team, from left to right, are (first row) Loretta Rush, Pauline Paloney, Joan Pavola, and Jeanette Neiderland; (second row) coach Joyce Brotland, Loraine Butts, Patsy Roundtree, Joy Allen, and Helen Lucas; (third row) Agnes Gensor, Margaret Zevecky, Nancy Mallinson, Velma Penyock, and Irene Neiderland.

The Sugar Creek School's full-time school nurse is seen in this May 1940 photograph. Nurse Swain would tend to student needs during the school day and help deliver the various services provided at the health clinic sponsored by the board of education and City of Sugar Creek that was held at the Sugar Creek City Hall.

After World War II, many Sugar Creek School students participated in the U.S. Department of the Treasury savings bond program designed to help meet the needs of disabled veterans. This certificate was given to Marjorie Ann Allen for her purchases in the school savings program in 1946. Sugar Creek residents had a history of buying war bonds, with total purchases of more than $65,000 in 1943 and over $172,000 in 1944.

The

UNITED STATES TREASURY DEPARTMENT

SAVINGS BONDS DIVISION

Certificate

In Recognition of the patriotic assistance given to the Rehabilitation and Hospitalization of our disabled veterans and the maintenance of our Forces of Occupation in the interest of Peace by

MARJORIE ANN ALLEN

through regular purchases of U. S. Savings Bonds and Stamps in the School Savings Program, this Certificate is awarded as an expression of the appreciation of the Treasury Department, the Veterans Administration and the Armed Forces of the United States of America.

CHIEF OF STAFF, U. S. ARMY   DIRECTOR, U. S. SAVINGS BONDS DIVISION FOR MISSOURI

ADMINISTRATOR OF VETERANS AFFAIRS   DIRECTOR, SCHOOLS SECTION, U. S. SAVINGS BONDS DIVISION FOR MISSOURI

MID-STATE PRINTING CO., JEFFERSON CITY, MO. 2335

Players on the 1946–1947 Sugar Creek School girls' basketball team are, from left to right, (first row) Beverly Beal, Norma Jean Palmer and Genevieve Neiderland; (second row) coach Weaver, Theresa Lucas, Betty Ann Manners, and Mary Agnes Pavola; (third row) Barbara Coleman, Elva Sutton, and Shirley Martinovich.

One of the more popular student activities at the Sugar Creek School was the girls' pep club. Cheerleaders and pep club members for the 1951–1952 school year are, from left to right, (first row) Doris Decker, Carole Roper, and Sue Lamb; (second row) teacher Mrs. Herre, Carol Ward, Betty Jude, Judee Gard, and Martha Pittello; (third row) Petra Pedrosa, Vicki Pyle, Carol Bartow, Donna Troutman, Gay Harris, Gwen Kendrick, and Janice Manners; (fourth row) Peggy Juricak, Sylvia Beal, Barbara Kiser, Cecilia Lonzo, Mary Sue Diesko, and Emily Halastik; (fifth row) Pat Hysell, Joann Dumsky, Mary Ann Allred, Bonnie Yates, and Dorothy Brashear.

Members of the Sugar Creek Board of Education are meeting to discuss the school district's business and the need for improvements to the old school buildings sometime before 1950. The men seated around the table are, clockwise from left to right, H. Ray Simms (vice president), Bob Allen (president), Virgil Lynch, John Gavin (secretary), Henry Pennington, J. Raymond Guy (superintendent), Andy Manners, and John Rozgay. Guy served as building principal and superintendent for more than 20 years from 1933 to 1956, except for a two-year span during 1943–1945 when he was in the navy. He provided the leadership to get a bond issue passed for a new elementary school, oversaw its construction, and served as principal of the building as well as the Carlisle School after the Sugar Creek district's merger with the Kansas City School District in 1956.

Marjorie Allen was awarded a certificate of appreciation from the Automobile Club of Missouri for her service in the Sugar Creek School's safety patrol in 1951. Her certificate was signed by principal J. Raymond Guy and teacher Irene Renner. Renner had a profound impact on many of her students, including the author of this book, when she taught civics and history classes at Van Horn High School.

Students are lined up to enter the new Sugar Creek School on the first day of the 1956–1957 school year. The building was a state-of-the-art school constructed after voters approved a $620,000 bond issue in 1953. In 1955, school district residents voted to join the Kansas City School District, and the merger became official on May 11. Sugar Creek's schools would remain in the Kansas City system for more than 50 years until a 2007 vote transferred them to the Independence School District.

Roger Hooper (left) and Jody Eaton were named the king and queen of the Sugar Creek School's Spring Carnival held during April 1964. Both youngsters would grow up and become members and officers of the Friends of Sugar Creek nonprofit group that developed the Sugar Creek Historical Center.

The Sugar Creek School's 1921 expansion to the original schoolhouse built in 1906 was destroyed by an arsonist's fire in 1980. At the time of the fire, the building was being used as a storage facility for city records and the Civic Relief Commission and as a practice room for the Sugar Creek Tamburitzans music group. Classes for elementary school students had not been held in the building since the new grade school opened in 1956.

Five

TENDING SOULS

During Jackson County's early history, Independence and Kansas City offered a variety of churches for Sugar Creek's farming community. Many of the ethnic workers who had come to town to build the Standard Oil refinery were Catholics who either attended St. Mary's Catholic Church in Independence or traveled to Kansas City, Kansas, for services in their native Croatian and other Slavic languages.

The first church to be established in Sugar Creek was the Methodist Episcopal Church, which met in the home of Col. N. P. Simonds from 1904 to 1907. Simonds, a Kansas City grain merchant, owned several lots in the northern part of town and another building used by the Methodists from 1908 to 1928. During 1928, the congregation moved into a new church at the corner of Norledge and Sterling Avenues.

St. Cyril's Catholic Church began in 1908 when the Sugar Creek Township Company donated five lots near the corner of Chicago and Cowan Streets. Construction started in 1909, and the first mass was held in 1914. The congregation later built a larger church that was dedicated in 1927.

The St. Joseph Greek Catholic Church was established in 1911, when meetings began once a month in a basement church started as a mission of a Kansas City, Kansas, Eastern Rite Catholic church. Most of the members of the congregation were immigrants from Austria, Bohemia, Slovakia, and Hungary who met in the basement church until 1925. A larger building constructed on the same site was completed in 1926, but the congregation continued to have monthly meetings until 1955. The arrival of a Ukrainian priest in 1955 enabled the church to have services every Sunday.

Prayer meetings for the Sugar Creek Church of God were held in homes and stores for several years starting in 1920. The congregation purchased a house for the church in 1941 and completed a new building in 1948. In 1965, a new sanctuary was completed on the same site after the original building was razed.

The fifth church established in Sugar Creek was the Reorganized Church of Jesus Christ of Latter Day Saints. Even though members of the church began meeting in Sugar Creek in 1925, the church was not officially established until 1929. Services were held in homes, community halls, and a former tavern over the next 10 years. In 1938, the congregation purchased a former grocery store at the corner of Kentucky Avenue and Northern Boulevard that served as their home until the 1970s.

Over the years, religious diversity in Sugar Creek has grown as the town's population and size has increased. The city is now home to several churches representing many denominations of faith.

Sugar Creek Methodist Church held its first services in 1904 at the summer home owned by Col. N. P. Simonds, a Kansas City grain merchant who had land in the north part of the town site. In 1908, Simonds constructed this building at the corner of High and Elizabeth Streets for the congregation's services. The church bought Simonds's building for $1,100 in 1917 and continued to worship in it until a new structure was completed in 1928. (Laurel Ann Bonine.)

The Sugar Creek Church of God held prayer meetings in member homes and a hotel room before having worship services regularly in a store at 713 Sterling Avenue sometime before 1938. The congregation, seen here in a 1920s photograph, bought a house five blocks further south at 211 Sterling Avenue from members Eva and William Frohman in 1941. Services were held in that house until 1948.

In 1908, the Sugar Creek Townsite Company donated five lots near the Riverview School for a church to be built for Sugar Creek's growing ethnic Catholic population. St. Cyril's Parish, named for the patron saint of the Slavic peoples, was formed, and construction was started on a 60-foot-by-36-foot basement church at the corner of Chicago and Cowan Streets. Between 1914 and 1927, the congregation grew, and the church became increasingly too small over time. The cornerstone for this semi-Gothic church, built over the basement church, was laid on October 31, 1926. Bishop Thomas Lillis dedicated the completed church on August 21, 1927. On Sunday afternoons, children learned to say the rosary and Litany of the Saints in Slovakian, the native tongue for many families in the congregation.

In 1927, the interior of St. Cyril's Church, seen in the photograph above, reflects the modest and humble nature of the Catholic Slavic immigrants. Pews were paid for by family subscriptions, the church bell and the Stations of the Cross on the walls were donated by the Zenska Jednota Slavic Ladies Union, and the church was cleaned each week by parish women. By 1946, the date of the photograph below, several changes had been made in the church interior, but the altar, stained-glass windows, and much of the statuary from the early years of the church remains. Families from many ethnicities and cultures have greatly added to the church and its cultural heritage.

Marriage ceremonies have been important events in Sugar Creek churches. This photograph was taken after a 1930 marriage. The happy celebrants are, from left to right, (first row) Al Stovich, Katie Bello, Louise Clemens, Ann Clemens, Anna Berislavich, Alice Benich, and Mary Stevens; (second row) John Salva, Andy Benich, Pete Dumsky, Joe Dumsky, and Hank Clemens.

By the mid-1920s, the congregation of St. Cyril's Catholic Church had more than 75 families, including several of Irish, Slovenian, and Hungarian descent. This photograph, taken outside the church around 1925, shows the clergy with unidentified boys and girls on their confirmation day standing with the proud members of their families.

Many early immigrants who came to work at the Standard Oil refinery were Eastern Rite Ukrainian Catholics from Austria, Hungary, and other eastern European countries. They began construction of a basement church on Chicago Street in 1911. The congregation of St. Joseph Greek Catholic Church attended services at a Kansas City, Kansas, church for three weeks and worshiped in their basement church once a month. During the 1920s, additional eastern European immigrants arrived in Sugar Creek and joined the congregation. Construction of a sanctuary over the basement church began in July 1925 and was completed a year later. The finished church is seen here in a photograph taken sometime between 1955 and 1958 when Rev. John Lazur, a Ukrainian priest, was pastor. Starting with Father Lazur's arrival, services have been held every Sunday and on holy days at the church.

Students of Sr. Mary David gave a musical recital at St. Cyril's Catholic Church in 1929 or 1930, only months after the church was dedicated. The performers are, from left to right, Mary Butkovich, Mary Ellen Gavin, Margaret Beal, John Gavin, Julia Frances Gavin, and Mary Tapko, with Elizabeth Clinton seated at the piano; the two children in front are unknown.

The first Catholic Slovak Ladies Union chapter of the Zenska Jednota was formed in 1914 at St. Cyril's Catholic Church. The women's lodge group was established to help meet the needs of immigrant families. Celebrating the golden jubilee of the group in 1964 are, from left to right, (first row) Barbara Kobe, Mary Beal, Monsignor A. F. Radwich, Theresa Wrabec, and Rev. Roman Malkowski; (second row) Helen Roper, Eva Slanko, Elizabeth Lipovsky (national president), Mary Pallo, and Anna Novak; (third row) Helen Brudzinski, Elizabeth Javorek, Mandica Butkovich, and Mildred Tapko.

This photograph captures the happy participants in a wartime wedding in Sugar Creek. Members of the wedding party are, from left to right, John Osipik, Edward Diesko, Joseph Wrabec, Edward Bootko, Bernice Diesko, Susie Haluska, Florence Bootko, and Irene Neiderland.

Following their initiation on July 20, 1951, sixty unidentified men became members of the local Knights of Columbus Council 3430. Most of the men were members of either St. Ann's in Fairmount, St. Mary's in Independence, or Sugar Creek's St. Cyril's Church. The group held meetings at the Gilpin Elementary School building on River Boulevard before it became inactive sometime in the late 1990s.

Construction of this building for the Church of God was started in 1947 on the same site as the Frohman house, which had served the congregation from 1941 to 1948. This new church, seen in the photograph above, was dedicated in September 1948. A parsonage was built in 1953, and the congregation started a 10-year effort to rebuild their church. This photograph was taken sometime between 1954 and 1958 when Rev. E. H. Tharp was pastor. The Church of God's new building, seen in the photograph below, was completed in 1965. Much of the original building on the site was torn down, but parts of the older church were incorporated into the new structure.

Even though the Reorganized Church of Jesus Christ of Latter Day Saints (now the Community of Christ) has long had its world headquarters in nearby Independence, efforts to form a branch of the church in Sugar Creek did not begin until 1925. Meetings were first held in homes, then moved to rented rooms in Chaney Hall and Slyman Hall on Sterling Avenue, and finally into the former Do Drop Inn. In 1939, the congregation purchased the grocery store owned by L. G. Lynch and converted it into the church seen in this photograph taken in 1957 when elder Myron Hershey was pastor.

The RLDS congregation continued holding services in their building at the corner of Kentucky Avenue and Northern Boulevard until the late 1970s. The church seen in this 1970 photograph was torn down and replaced with a new church on the same site. By the early 1990s, the RLDS congregation grew small and sold the building to the Church of Christ.

86

Fr. A. F. Radwich stands behind some of the youngest members of St Cyril's congregation in this c. 1960 photograph. The children from left to right are Sharon Smitka, Marilyn Maglich, Karen Fries, Tina Manners, Pam Russell, Ron Martinovich, John Russell, Terry Smitka, John Ham, Joe Topi, and Cathleen Calovich.

Rev. A. F. Radwich of St. Cyril's Catholic Church is honored with a banquet celebrating his 25th anniversary in the priesthood in this 1961 photograph. Reverend Radwich had succeeded Fr. P. M. Smith, who had worked to build the church. The reverend left the church in 1960 when he was elevated to the position of monsignor. Standing alongside Father Radwich (center) are John Kroll (left) and John Lubek (right).

The congregation of Sugar Creek Methodist Church bought this lot at the corner of Sterling and Norledge Streets and began constructing a new church on July 30, 1928. Services were held at the Odd Fellows' Hall for nearly five months until the church building was ready for worship. This picture of the church was taken sometime before 1958 when the Reverend Harry B. Davis was pastor.

Six

STANDARD OIL

John D. Rockefeller formed Standard Oil as an Ohio corporation in 1870 when he was 31 years old. He and his partners used highly effective, albeit ruthless, tactics to build the company into a fully integrated oil producing, transporting, refining, and marketing combine. By 1882, the several companies that were part of the enterprise were combined into a business trust that continued to grow by increasing sales and acquiring competing firms. The company's aggressive activities and secret deals with railroads attracted the attention of a number of state legislatures and, after Congress passed the Sherman Antitrust Act in 1890, the federal government.

In 1889, Rockefeller formed Standard Oil of Indiana as part of his trust. This venture was located at a single oil production facility outside Whiting, Indiana, and refined oil into axle grease for industrial machinery, paraffin wax for candles, and kerosene for home lighting. By 1903, the trust's refinery at Neodasha, Kansas, could not refine oil as fast as it was coming out of the Kansas and Oklahoma oil fields. The company decided to build another refinery in Sugar Creek and transport oil through a pipeline to the new plant. Standard Oil brought key personnel from the Whiting facility to oversee construction and begin refining the crude oil. More than 600 men were hired to build the plant. By October 1904, the facility was able to produce its first batch of kerosene.

The refinery and its management had a major impact and important role in Sugar Creek's early development. Local businesses grew to meet the needs of the company's employees, managers became city officials and political leaders, and taxes the company paid helped finance the community's endeavors. Most of Sugar Creek's streets were named after people who were attached to the refinery.

In 1911, the Standard Oil trust was broken up by the U. S. Supreme Court, and Standard Oil of Indiana became an independent company. The company bought an interest in the American Oil Company in 1925 and in 1973 decided to make Amoco its national brand. In 1998, Amoco merged with British Petroleum, or BP.

Over the years in Sugar Creek, the refinery grew from its original 70 acres to more than 450 acres and increased its refining capacity from less than 6,000 barrels of crude oil per day to nearly 110,000 barrels a day. Amoco announced it would discontinue its Sugar Creek refinery in June 1982 because of declining demand for petroleum products in the United States. Most of the storage tanks, process equipment, and buildings were demolished by 1989, but a bulk storage unit and an asphalt plant were kept in operation.

The first local employees hired in 1903 to begin constructing Standard Oil's Sugar Creek refinery were Joe Bostian, Magnus Erickson, J. A. Hininger, and A. E. Nylund. During 1904, an additional 963 men were hired to build and operate the plant, bringing more than $30,000 a month into the local economy. Initial facilities at the refinery included an office building, a boiler shop, machine shop, blacksmith shop, pipe shop, gas plant, and waterworks that used as many as 20 million gallons of Missouri River water to power the operation by summer 1905. A large tank farm was built to store thousands of barrels of crude oil being brought to the refinery by the pipeline from Neodasha, Kansas. Most of the stills used to produce kerosene were located along the Atchison, Topeka and Santa Fe Railway tracks at the north end of the refinery. This photograph, taken in 1904 or 1905, shows the company's office and laboratory, several of the receiving storage tanks, a portion of the railroad yard, and tank cars used by the Sugar Creek and Maywood Railway to carry refined products to markets throughout the Midwest.

John D. Rockefeller, seen here at the age of 74 in a 1913 photograph, hardly seems to be the ruthless businessman who stimulated public and government attacks on Standard Oil that began almost immediately after Congress passed the Sherman Antitrust Act in 1890. He distributed power and policy making to committees at the company's main offices, first in Cleveland and then in New York City. Rockefeller retired from the company in 1897 but remained a major shareholder. (Library of Congress, Prints and Photographs Division.)

In 1905, Missouri sued Standard Oil for operating in violation of antitrust laws, seeking to prohibit it from operating in the state. Four years later, company attorneys proposed Standard and Missouri form a corporation to administer trust holdings. This 1909 *Chicago Daily News* cartoon by Luther Bradley portrays suspicions of state officials: Standard Oil is an octopus bent into the shape of a Trojan horse. In 1911, the U.S. Supreme Court broke Standard Oil into 34 companies. (Library of Congress, Prints and Photographs Division.)

By 1911, the Standard Oil trust controlled 80 percent of American crude oil, 80 percent of all kerosene, and 90 percent of all lubricating oils. It owned half of all railroad tank cars, sold 300 million candles, and operated a fleet of 78 steamships and 19 sailing ships. The daily production from nearly

This photograph of the refinery, looking from the partially developed hillside west of the facility to the east, was taken sometime between 1910 and 1912. The long building in the foreground is the refinery's first machine shop, and the initial group of crude oil storage tanks is at the center and right. Each of these storage tanks had a capacity of 190,000 barrels of crude oil, all piped from Kansas and Oklahoma oil fields.

92

10,000 barrels of crude oil at the Sugar Creek refinery, seen here in a 1909 panoramic image looking northward toward the Missouri River, was primarily kerosene. Production shifted more to gasoline as the use of automobiles grew. (Library of Congress, Prints and Photographs Division.)

A companion view of the refinery taken between 1910 and 1912 shows the first powerhouse in the right foreground and the six short smokestacks of the early batch stills at the center next to the railway siding close to the Missouri River. Land for expansion of the refinery was purchased in 1910 but not developed because the company did not know what the Missouri state government would do about federal antitrust court actions against the trust. The refinery's first expansion came when additional storage tanks were built on the west and south sides of the plant between 1912 and 1915.

Two Standard Oil refinery trucks are parked outside the main entrance and south facade of Kansas City's Union Station. Construction of the terminal began in 1910 and was nearing completion when this photograph was taken a few weeks before the station opened to the public in October 1914. By rail, a passenger traveled 8.6 miles to make the trip between the new Union Station and the Atchison, Topeka and Santa Fe Railway's Sugar Creek depot.

This 1920 photograph shows eight unknown batch still cleaners next to a rail hopper. The men would climb into the stills with shovels, picks, and scoopers attached to their gloved hands to scrape burned coke residue left on the tank's walls after the initial fractioning of crude oil. They wore thick wooden shoes to help protect their feet from the hot coke and walls that had temperatures around 130 to 140 degrees when the men worked inside.

Standard Oil began having company picnics for employees and their families in the early 1920s. This photograph shows contestants taking part in a three-legged race during the 1924 event held in June on the grounds of nearby Fairmount Park.

The company sponsored the Standard Oil Athletic and Social Club for employees to participate in a wide variety of sports, hobbies, and social activities. This photograph shows proud members of the company championship basketball team for 1925. The players on the "Office" team are, from left to right, Roy Jones, Mike Kobe, Kenneth Jackson, ? Jett, Farmer Frisbey, and coach Earl Cox.

The refinery's rail yard, next to the company office in this 1926 photograph, is filled with tank cars owned by the Union Tank Car Company. The tank car company had been a subsidiary of Standard Oil from 1891 until the trust was broken in 1911 and transported most of the oil products produced at the refinery. In 1926, the Sugar Creek town council renamed Hackett Street as Felton Street to honor the contributions of Henry E. Felton, president of the Union Tank Car Company. (Richard N. Piland.)

The Standard Oil Refinery Band poses for this photograph as it participates in the parade marking the centennial of neighboring Independence on October 5, 1927. The popular band had nine charter members when it was formed in 1919 and grew to 18 musicians when the group gave its first Christmas concert on December 24, 1919. Weekly concerts were held in the bandstand in the company park or at the Riverview School auditorium and usually lasted one hour, with the band playing mostly marches and patriotic music.

During the late 1920s, refinery employees parked their cars along Sterling Avenue, which led to the plant's main gate entrance marked by the small shack beyond the last group of vehicles. The brick building and storage tanks to the left indicate the terminal where tanker trucks were loaded with coal oil or gasoline. The refinery band often performed concerts in the small pavilion that can be seen beyond the trees in the park area to the left of the street. (Laurel Ann Bonine.)

This 1930s image shows the stabilizer tower that added material to keep gasoline from souring, or losing octane. In the background beyond the refinery are two structures of note: the two-story building at the left is the Standard Hotel, built by N. P. Simonds in 1906 where Elizabeth Street intersected with Fairmount Avenue; on the right is the F. P. Gavin confectionery and grocery store that opened in 1919.

During the 1930s, much of the heavier residue produced from refining crude oil in Sugar Creek was sent to other Standard Oil refineries. This photograph from 1938 shows the area and loading dock on the Missouri River where barges would take on tons of black oil residue for shipping to the company's refinery in Wood River, Illinois, or the original Whiting, Indiana, location where it would be made into asphalt.

Members of the refinery's Main Office Whisker Club pose for this photograph before they take part in the second Santa-Cali-Gon Festival in Independence in 1947. Participants in the celebration honoring the three trails to the west are, from left to right, (first row) Albert Akers, Joseph Pinson, Roy Frazer, Elbert Mock, Joe Yates, and Jim Bridges; (second row) Pete Mikulich, Chester Haukenberry, Oscar Hock, William Mengle, Wayne Zion, and Ed Chandler; (third row) Maynard Sands, F. O. Blake, Russell Keck, Forest Green, and Elbert Yates; (fourth row) Cecil Smith, H. D. McPherson, Lambert Patrick, and Dennis Bowman; (fifth row) W. C. Moore, Larry Veuleman, Leonard Yates, Guy Hurshman, and J. W. Campbell; (sixth row) Otis Mitchell, Harvey Dutzel, and Earl Lynd.

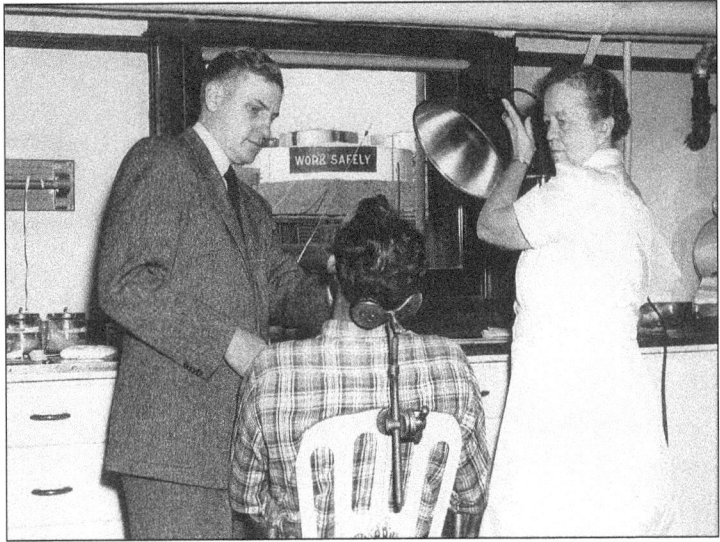

Refinery employees were frequently urged to prevent accidents and preserve their health. The plant had a small infirmary to provide prompt first-aid to workers. In this photograph from the late 1940s, Dr. Richard Green (left) and nurse Myrtle Taylor tend to an unidentified employee.

As part of a celebration of the refinery's 50th anniversary in 1954, several longtime employees stand next to a horse-drawn tank wagon that delivered the refinery's kerosene to its customers in 1904. Directly behind the flatbed truck holding the tank wagon is a more modern tanker truck. The six retirees in the picture are, from left to right, Bert Wesner, Ashton B. Jones, Ben F. Payne, H. R. Boehmer, H. J. Hininger, and Curtis Wright.

The first new crude oil refining technique used at Sugar Creek was thermal cracking, a process using high temperatures and pressure in specially designed stills that was invented in 1912 by William Burton and Robert Humphreys, two Standard Oil of Indiana chemists. In 1937, French inventor Eugene Houdry added a clay catalyst to the process and greatly increased the quality and yield of gasoline. By the early 1940s, Standard Oil built the fluid catalytic cracking unit (above) to convert crude into high-octane gasoline and other distillate fuels. The 16-story "cat cracker" had a capacity 400 times that of the old Burton thermal stills and used less heat and pressure at a greater speed. Refining operations are regulated by instruments in the control room of the fluid catalytic cracker unit (below). The two process men monitoring instruments are not known.

Frank Roper (left) and Abe Onka were working at the blender manifold when this photograph was taken sometime around 1950. The men are mixing the components needed for a particular product such as seasonally balanced gasoline, kerosene, or aircraft fuel and preparing it for final distribution. The building to the right is part of the refinery's blender unit. St. Cyril's Catholic Church can be seen in the distance to the left center in the photograph.

These two tall flare stacks standing near the Missouri River were almost always burning excess light ends or gases that could not be processed during the refining of crude oil. They also served a pressure release safety function whenever there were problems at the catalytic cracker. At those times, problem vapors were sent to the flare stacks for burning. After the company built a vapor recovery unit, most of the unprocessed gases were turned into liquid gases such as butane and propane.

Fires were relatively frequent events at the refinery, especially as technologies and manufacturing processes changed. The plant's fire department, first formed in January 1905, also responded to fires in the community such as those that destroyed George Rodman's saloon in 1908 and burned a combined lunchroom and pool hall operated by Sherry Simpson in 1913. Firefighters were kept busy in 1917 when five new Burton thermal stills started a fire in November and in December when 20 stills exploded, sending flames high in the sky. A spectacular fire in 1937 resulted when a loaded railroad tank car crashed into a locomotive near the Crawford entrance to the refinery. The fire in this undated photograph occurred among the older batch stills at the north end of the refinery. The Atchison, Topeka and Santa Fe's railroad tracks and the Missouri River can be seen just beyond the smoke in the center of the picture.

This accident prevention award was given to workers at the refinery's fluid catalytic cracker unit by the American Petroleum Institute in 1963. Received by foreman Joe Topi on behalf of the staff, it honored the employees for working 819,260 man-hours without a disabling injury during the nearly 15-year period from July 6, 1948, to February 28, 1963. The actual number of man-hours the staff worked without an accident was 913,260. (Steve Topi.)

The first community-wide Independence Day celebration in Sugar Creek was held in 1940 when several businessmen sponsored a holiday observance. The group organizing the event became the Sugar Creek Business and Professional Club. This c. 1960 photograph shows the company's first-place prize-winning float carrying five daughters of refinery employees. The girls on the float are, from left to right, Pamela Kluska, Mary Frances Rozgay, Maureen Padgett, Sandra Stockton, and Karen Sue Vajda.

In this 1955 photograph, four company managers receive training on how to run the new ultraformer unit at the refinery. The unit further refined oil hydrocarbons into lighter, more valuable products after the crude was processed at the fluid catalytic cracker facility. The men studying the reforming unit are, from left to right, Dick Nottage, George Weis, Pete Anderson, and C. W. Smith.

This view of the north end of the refinery shows the water intake and water treatment facilities along the Missouri River; the Atchison, Topeka and Santa Fe Railway tracks; power station 16 on the right; several steam and flare lines; and the continuous crude stills near the center. In the distance in the center of the image are the tall smokestacks and towers that are part of the Missouri Portland Cement operation in Cement City.

Refinery employees are seen during a shift change at the main gate and clock house in this photograph taken in 1957 or 1958. In 1957, the refinery employed more than 1,175 people over three shifts and had a yearly payroll of more than $8 million. For many employees, a job at the refinery represented long-term financial security for their families. In 1953, more than 550 people had been with the company for 10 years or longer, more than 125 had worked for 30 years or more, and 11 had been employed for more than 40 years.

Several refinery employees are seen loading a company tanker truck with gasoline for delivery to area service stations in this photograph from the late 1950s. The company operated product pipelines that carried most of the refinery's output to terminals in Iowa, Illinois, and South Dakota. Railroad tank cars and transport truckers carried the remainder of the refinery's products directly to customers or to bulk storage terminals in Missouri and Kansas.

The company's new Administration, Engineering, and Research Building located on Kentucky Avenue is seen in this 1953 photograph. Chemists, physicists, chemical engineers, and technicians in this building worked to develop new and improved products and processes, tested components and products for quality, and created projects to increase the operating efficiency of the refinery. Departments such as accounting, human resources, and other general headquarters functions were also housed in the building.

The refinery experienced strikes in 1919, 1921, and several other years. Some of the company's employees and members of their families are walking a picket line outside the plant's main entrance during an eight-month strike in 1958. The work stoppage brought production at the plant to a complete standstill. The long walkout was a very bitter and divisive period for the community; families were torn apart, businesses suffered, relationships among neighbors were strained, and city resources were depleted. Less than half of the union workers were called back to work at the refinery after the strike.

Over the years, refinery personnel were actively involved in a variety of community activities and organizations. This 1961 photograph shows a meeting featuring several company executives and representatives of the United Campaign that was held to request a group of employees to make a "fair share" contribution of one hour's pay per month to the fund. Many workers must have made a donation because the banner on the wall indicates 90 percent to 100 percent participation for the 1960 campaign.

E. Lee Comer, mayor of Independence, designated October 7, 1979, as "American Oil Company Day" in his city with the proclamation seen here. The mayor acknowledged the Sugar Creek refinery's 75 years of existence, its friendship and support for Independence's cultural, economic, and civic activities, and the hundreds of jobs it provided residents. Less than three years later, Amoco closed its refinery because of declining demand for petroleum products.

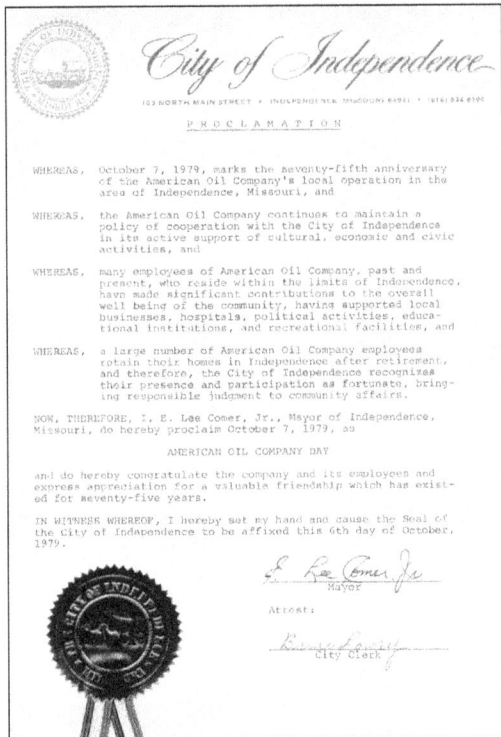

This 1962 aerial photograph of the refinery provides a clear view of the scope of the Standard Oil Company's operation at the plant during its peak years. The facility covered more than 430 acres, processed about 110,000 barrels of crude oil every day, and employed as many as 1,600 people. The Sugar Creek depot of the Atchison, Topeka and Santa Fe Railway is to the lower center edge of the image, and the water intake and purification facilities are to the lower right. To the far left are the east storage tank area, asphalt terminal, and the administration, engineering, and research office building. Beyond the Kansas City Southern track and tank car loading platforms are the three tank-farm areas surrounding the major refinery facilities. Amoco ceased its refinery operations in June 1982, and most of the tanks, process equipment, and buildings were demolished in 1989. The loss was difficult for the Sugar Creek community. In 1982, Amoco paid local taxes totaling more than $835,000. By 1986, the total was about $55,000. (Steve Topi.)

Seven

COMMUNITY LIFE

Sugar Creek residents have had a variety of opportunities to enjoy the lifestyles they have wanted for themselves and their families. The community and surrounding area offer residents a high quality of life. For most residents, life in Sugar Creek centers around families, the town's churches, schools, ethnic heritages, and social organizations. As might be expected, for many years much of the community's well-being was dependent on the Standard Oil refinery. After the plant ceased operations, residents adapted to the loss and town leaders worked to create a positive outcome and settlement of a multimillion-dollar lawsuit with BP over contamination caused by the refinery.

Community-wide activities and several festivals have been staged in Sugar Creek for many years. Slavic folk festivals and citywide folk dances have been held since the 1970s, first sponsored by St Cyril's Parish and then by many local organizations including the Moose Lodge, the Veterans of Foreign Wars, the Eagles, the Optimists, Knights of Columbus, and St. Cyril's Church. Young people have been involved in the Sugar Creek Tamburitzan musical group since it was formed in 1969 and have entertained many residents with their performances of ethnic music played on instruments made by hand or brought to the town by Slavic immigrants. In 1976, the group traveled to Washington, D.C., and performed before an international audience attending an Optimist International convention.

There have been several fraternal and civic groups that have worked to improve the quality of life for Sugar Creek residents as well as provide for the social needs of their members. Over the years, many aspects of life in town have been improved by the work done by groups such as the Sugar Creek Improvement Association and the Sugar Creek Business and Professional Club. Many young people have taken part in a wide variety of youth programs. The town has had a very successful youth baseball program for many years. Youngsters have been involved in Scouting programs since the first troop was established in 1920. Several other recreational activities have centered around the Sugar Creek Municipal Pool during the years from 1955 to the early 1990s. One of the most popular of those activities was the annual Sugar Creek Beauty Queen competition.

The city government, working with local benefactors and organizations, has developed acres of parklands and recreational facilities for the enjoyment of the town's residents. Today there are community-owned tennis courts, baseball fields, a football field, several excellent parks, and a community center for banquets and meetings.

Sugar Creek has retained the advantages of small-town living with quiet residential areas, nice recreational facilities and parklands, decent streets, good fire and police protection, and a friendly sense of community and spirit. These characteristics have built the solid foundation upon which the town will continue to be a special place where life is a little sweeter.

The town's first Boy Scout group was organized around 1918 by A. S. Hurt, superintendent and principal of the Riverview School. The troop was led by scoutmaster Rev. B. F. McCowan, pastor of the Sugar Creek Methodist Church, and his assistant, Shelton Huffman. This photograph of the young Scouts was taken outside the church located near the corner of High and Elizabeth Streets in 1920. By 1926, the group of boys was known as Troop 209, with teacher E. E. Frye as scoutmaster. (Laurel Ann Bonine.)

The 1929 Young Men's Christian Association baseball team is seen in this photograph taken at the Sugar Creek ball field. The members of the team are, from left to right, (first row) George Vida, Louie Husbenet, John Beal, Andy Maglich, and Tony Maglich; (second row) John Gavin, John Clemens, John Stevens, Andy Manners, Louie Fries, Blackie Rozgay, Chuck Farrand, and Guy McAvoy.

When this photograph was taken on December 1, 1936, thirty-one immigrants to the United States were attending an adult education citizenship class in the eighth-grade classroom at Sugar Creek School. The class, one of several Works Progress Administration programs in Sugar Creek during the Depression, was instructed by a Mr. Krulick, who is standing near the rear of the class.

Ellis Cairns organized Sugar Creek's first girls' softball team in 1938. The 1939 team seen in this photograph won 24 games, lost 9, and tied 1 during the season. Members of the Cairns Busters team are, from left to right, (first row) Lorene Allen, Doris Cairns, Dee Dee Cairns, Florence Singleton, and unknown; (second row) coach Mason Faulkerson, June Carey, Johanna Waller, Betty Meyers, Jo Sharp, Frances Freeman, and sponsor Ellis Cairns; (third row) Betty Frank Evinger, Anna Pallo, Helen Stelz, Frances Diesko, ? Larson, Iris Cairns, and Katie Zorich.

111

The October 6, 1941, "Blue Valley Tornado" touched down first at 43rd Street and Jackson Avenue in Kansas City, passed through the Van Horn and Fairmount areas, and struck Sugar Creek near Watertower Hill along Kentucky Avenue east of Sterling Avenue. The storm completely destroyed several homes and damaged dozens of others, causing property damage estimated at more than $25,000, with no loss of life. Jack Faulkner looks at his family's house after it had been picked up and moved 15 feet off its foundation by the storm.

Fairmount Avenue was resurfaced in 1925 after voters passed a bond issue by a vote of 150 to 50. The next year, Fairmount was renamed Sterling Avenue, and the city began using house numbers in local addresses. In 1941, another bond issue provided $119,000 for culverts, storm sewers, sidewalks, and street improvements such as widening Sterling and Kentucky Avenues and paving Gill, Chicago and Claremont Streets. This early photograph shows an unpaved Gill Street running from the bottom to the top of the photograph. The road leading off to the right is Forest Street.

Five members of Boy Scout Troop 268 received the rank of Eagle Scout in a Court of Honor ceremony in 1945. The young men who attained the honor are, from left to right, Jack O'Renick, Bob O'Renick, Robert Bateman, John Onka, and Jack Crouch. Troop 268 was sponsored by St. Cyril's Catholic Church.

The city purchased land along Kentucky Avenue for Sugar Creek Memorial Park in 1944. Residents voluntarily donated more than $1,600 to build the monument to the town's war dead that is seen in this 1956 photograph. The Memorial Park was dedicated during a special Decoration Day service in 1946. The chain fence visible to the far right in the background is part of the enclosure surrounding the municipal pool.

Sugar Creek's Edna Stillwell was a 16-year-old usherette at a Kansas City theater when she met 18-year-old comedian Red Skelton in 1930. After their marriage in 1931, she was his business manager and created some of his best-known routines and characters. This 1948 image at the Stillwell home in Independence shows, from left to right, (first row) Orville L. Stillwell, June Stillwell, Geraldine Stillwell, Edna Stillwell-Skelton, and Charles Stillwell; (second row) Doris Stillwell, Ruth Stillwell, Richard "Red" Skelton, and Orville G. Stillwell. (Doris Snyder.)

Sugar Creek's Sterling Rebekah Lodge No. 799 was formed in 1930. The group was one of the most active lodges in the Kansas City area and worked hard to provide for the Odd Fellows Home in Liberty, Missouri. The women who were officers for the 1949 year are, from left to right, (first row) Ada Evinger, Elva Sutton, Maud Sutton, Blanche Buford, Nina Frisbey, Blanche Evinger, and Flannie King; (second row) Martha Walden, Madge Pitt, Gladys Powell, Velma Thompson, Tillie Buford, Martha Crowl, Frances Craven, Essie Ohler, and Elizabeth Tarwater.

Mayor Rudy J. Roper buys the first Veterans of Foreign Wars Buddy Poppy from 11-year-old Judee Gard in this 1950 photograph. Seven years later, Judee would win the second annual Sugar Creek Beauty Queen contest held at the municipal pool.

Sugar Creek's annual Independence Day Parade route ran from the north end of Sterling Avenue to Independence Avenue, west to Northern Boulevard, and then north to the town baseball park. The celebration was held all day and into the late evening. This 1951 photograph was taken near the corner of Independence Avenue and Northern Boulevard shortly after parade participants passed a Hudson Oil Company station selling their regular grade of gasoline for 25.9¢ per gallon.

Voters approved a $100,000 bond issue in 1954 to finance the design and construction of the Sugar Creek Municipal Pool, one of the first community swimming pools in Jackson County. This 1955 photograph shows a group of unidentified bricklayers working to complete the interior of the primary entrance to the pool. The entrance faced the town's Memorial Park, which was on the west side of the pool. Dressing rooms and lockers for men were to the left of the entrance, and the women's changing rooms were located to the right.

Most of the swimming pool construction had been completed when this photograph was taken in May or June 1955. Workers had not yet installed the pool's diving boards, public benches, or completed the landscaping around the site. The pool was located on Kentucky Avenue, slightly west of the Kansas City Southern Railroad tracks and Sterling Avenue. The Standard Oil refinery dominates the view to the north of the site.

Sugar Creek Municipal Pool opened to the public on July 2, 1955. It was an immediate success, with more than 75,000 people using the pool during each of its first two seasons of operation in 1956 and 1957. "The hunky dunk" was a profitable, popular recreation center for residents of Sugar Creek and drew many people from nearby areas such as Fairmount, Maywood, Englewood, and other parts of Independence and Kansas City. The facility provided two wading pools for children, a 60-foot-by-120-foot main pool, three diving boards, a concession stand, dressing rooms, and lockers. The pool's staff provided swimming lessons for beginners and advanced classes in lifesaving and water safety. In 1956, the first Sugar Creek Beauty Queen contest was held at the pool, beginning an annual tradition that continued until the early 1990s. The city closed the pool in 1993 due to decreased attendance, low revenues, poor management, and high maintenance and repair costs. The entire swimming pool was completely dismantled and covered over in 1998.

Nancy Ann Adlard won the Miss Sugar Creek Beauty Queen contest in 1959. The event was the fourth held at municipal pool. Adlard was also chosen Miss Jackson County and represented the area in the 1959 Miss Missouri pageant. She frequently appeared in a variety of local newspaper and television advertisements for Mugs Up Root Beer and other area businesses. The first three winners of the town's beauty queen contest were Margaret Rozgay, Judee Gard, and Rose Ann Butkovich.

Robert F. Kennedy looks over a crowd of Sugar Creek Democrats during his September 24, 1960, campaign speech on behalf of the John F. Kennedy–Lyndon B. Johnson national ticket. The event at the town baseball field helped JFK win the popular vote in Jackson County by 19,280 votes. Kennedy carried Missouri by a slim margin of only 9,980 votes, defeating Republicans Richard M. Nixon and Henry Cabot Lodge, 50.3 percent to 49.7 percent. (Harry S. Truman Library.)

Democrats attending the Kennedy speech were also asked to support Edward V. Long, who had been appointed U.S. senator on September 23, 1960, and to vote for John M. Dalton and Hilary A. Bush, the party's nominees for Missouri governor and lieutenant governor. The three loyal Kennedy supporters offering attendees Pepsi, Schlitz, and Falstaff are, from left to right, Gladys Salva, Janice Andrisevic, and Bernice Manners. (Harry S. Truman Library.)

Sugar Creek's Betty Ann Manners was 18 when she joined the European touring cast of Holiday on Ice in 1949. She took part in shows until 1960. This photograph shows Manners dressed in a costume from one of the productions.

During the mid-1950s, the City of Sugar Creek bought a 10-acre tract of tax-delinquent land east of the city limits for future expansion and development. Ethel E. Harrison owned 10 acres adjacent to the tract and offered to donate her property if a large park would be created, and on January 1, 1958, the city annexed the acreage for a new park. This 1957 photograph was taken as a crane operator and his helpers begin hoisting one of the prefabricated concrete supports for a planned shelter into place on the prepared site. (Laurel Ann Bonine.)

A work crew from the Kansas City Concrete Company and crane operators continue to build the supporting structure for the shelter house. Other work to open roads into the parkland had to be done by the city to facilitate the upgrades. Development of the park, including improvements such as the shelter house, was supervised by Edwin C. "Pete" Saxton, the city's street and water superintendent. Saxton worked to gain the support of many local civic organizations for the park improvements. (Laurel Ann Bonine.)

The park was dedicated as the Sugar Creek-William Henry Harrison Memorial Park and officially opened for public use with the ceremony seen in these June 1, 1958, photographs. Harrison, who died in 1945, was the great-grandson of William Henry Harrison, the ninth president of the United States. The younger Harrison was a partner in a property development firm that traced its beginnings to 1871 and included Benjamin Harrison, the 23rd president of the United States, as an owner until the 1890s. The park's namesake had worked to build moderately priced residential developments throughout the Inter-City area, including major housing districts near the Centropolis and Sheffield industrial areas and the Standard Oil Company refinery. The platform guests and speakers at the dedication seen in the photograph below, from left to right, are H. M. Clements, Jacob Brown (head visible only), unknown (behind podium), Mayor Rudy J. Roper (at podium), P. C. Livesay, Edwin C. "Pete" Saxton, Bob Morton, Rev. A. F. Radwich, Steve J. Salva, unknown, Irene Neiderland, Virgil Lynch, Ethel E. Harrison, John E. Dumsky, and Anthony S. Jasso. (Both, Laurel Ann Bonine.)

The queen and princesses of the seventh annual Sugar Creek Beauty Queen contest pose poolside for this 1962 photograph. The lovely ladies are, from left to right, Joyce Wagner, Dee Ann Klaus (queen), and Mary Layton. All three of the popular women graduated from Van Horn High School.

Slavic customs and ethnic cultural traditions have been shared in celebrations involving many Sugar Creek residents through the years. Special meals and foods such as cabbage rolls, home-baked Povitica, kolache, and other fruit and nut confections were served at the festivities. This c. 1960 photograph shows Tootie (left) and Mattie Butkovich dressed in traditional Slavic dress and dancing a spirited polka.

The Sugar Creek Tamburitzans was founded in 1968 by Mattie Butkovich, Barry Berislavich, and Bob Pinter to teach Slavic and Croatian musical heritage to young people. The group, made up of 24 boys and girls aged 8 to 14 years old, dressed in authentic costumes, sang songs in Slavic languages, played tamburitzan instruments, and performed native Balkan dances. The members of the band in this 1971 photograph are, from left to right, (first row) Randy Novak, Mary Jo Maglich, Janice Butkovich, Patti Smitka, Kim Guthrie, and Mark O'Renick; (second row) Nick Rodina (director), Lisa Kolich, Ann Maglich, Pam Snow, Nick Andrisevic, Mark Pallo, John Berislavich, and Bob Pinter (cofounder); (third row) John Hix, Sharon Rodina, Philip Butkovich, Mark Petrovic, Mark Pinter, and Joe Salva; (fourth row) Barry Berislavich (cofounder), Ray Bukaty, Ed Kovac, Frank Kovac, Mark Tapko, Joe Ham, Bill Mikula, and Mattie Butkovich (cofounder). Many of the band's instruments were handmade by Nick Rodina, the group's director.

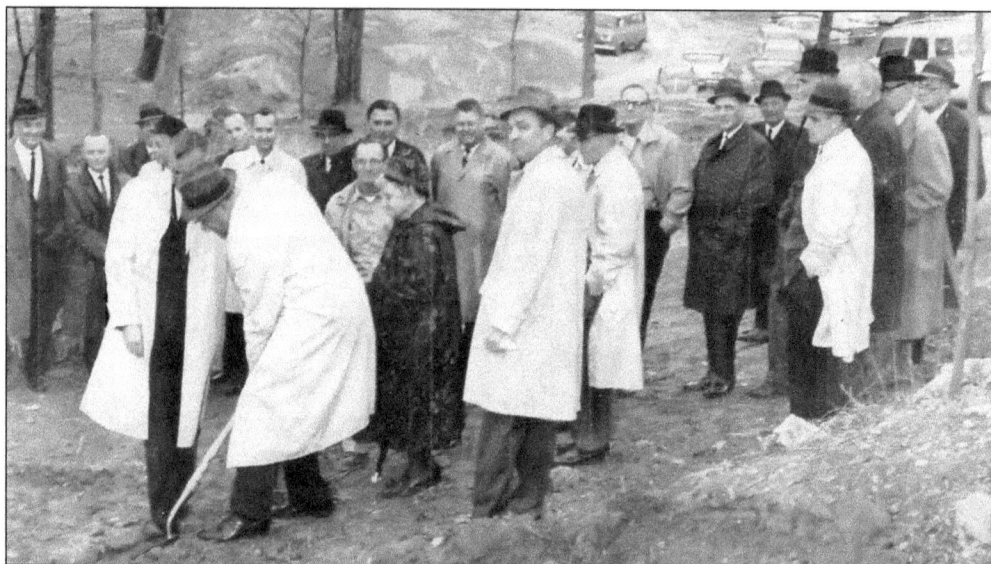

Mayor R. J. Roper turns the first shovel of dirt during the ground-breaking ceremony for a new community meeting place on March 9, 1966. The Sugar Creek Business and Professional Club, which had formed in 1940, spearheaded the project. Other participants included the Inter-City Optimist Club, American Oil Company, and other local organizations. Construction of the building, on a site next to William Henry Harrison Memorial Park, would take more than three years.

Area businesses donated much of the equipment and materials needed to construct the building. Hundreds of Sugar Creek residents devoted hours of free labor during weekend construction. In this photograph, six unidentified volunteers are working to set a door and lay bricks for the exterior walls during early stages of the building's construction in 1966 or 1967. (Laurel Ann Bonine.)

124

The community center was incomplete when Sugar Creek police chief Mike D. Onka was killed in the line of duty on February 5, 1968. Onka's death was a stimulus to community members, who pushed the new center to completion. In June 1969, the Mike D. Onka Memorial Building was dedicated. The blond brick building was equipped with kitchen facilities, a large banquet room, and other amenities that helped it become a center of community activities. (Laurel Ann Bonine.)

The large community meeting room at the Mike D. Onka Memorial Building is nearly ready for the banquet on April 19, 1970, marking the start of festivities for Sugar Creek's 50th anniversary. The dinner was prepared and served by the women of the Mike Onka Memorial Auxiliary. More than 450 guests, including 28 local couples who had been married for more than 50 years, enjoyed a fine meal and were entertained by the Sugar Creek Tamburitzans, who performed a program of Croatian and Czechoslovakian folk music.

Sugar Creek's Marsha Kolich was a national finalist when she represented Missouri in the 1976 Miss America pageant. She had won the Miss Jackson County and Miss Missouri contests before appearing in the Atlantic City, New Jersey, pageant hosted by Bert Parks and Phyllis George. In 1974, she had won the Miss Independence contest.

Members of the Sugar Creek Tamburitzan band, their parents, and other Sugar Creek residents pose in front of the United States Capitol in this 1976 photograph. The band members traveled to Washington, D.C., to perform at the 58th annual convention of the Optimist International Club at the request of the Inter-City Optimist Club of Sugar Creek.

The city purchased the land for the town baseball field after a $15,000 bond was approved by voters in 1941. Funds also paid for grading and enlarging the ballpark. This 1982 photograph of the shelter house and ball field shows the new electronic scoreboard erected when the facility was renamed R. J. Roper Stadium to honor the mayor for 40 years of service.

Edwin C. "Pete" Saxton proudly displays cabbages he raised in his family garden in this c. 1980 photograph. Saxton, who served the town as street and water commissioner from 1943 to the early 1970s, supervised the effort to develop William Henry Harrison Memorial Park, including the dedication ceremony in 1958. The dog under the table is Brownie, a neighbor's pet who adopted Saxton and stayed by his side.

Visit us at
arcadiapublishing.com

· ·